Praise for Crossing the Bridge

"As a psychotherapist, I found this book to be a useful and highly specific instruction manual for both laypeople and therapists/coaches to empower individuals to cultivate deeper connections. It fills a niche in the field that is currently devoid of specificity. I appreciated the plethora of concrete verbal strategies and purposeful skills that were particularly applicable in clinical settings. The book is infused with Trime's lived experience, which adds depth and color. A great addition to my therapist bookshelf!"

—Michele Lonergan, LPC, NCC, CNEP

"When Trime Persinger felt dismissed in my rather rude email exchange, she could have walked away. Instead, she demonstrated the very skills she teaches—reaching back across the divide with curiosity instead of defensiveness, sharing thoughtful research to bridge our differences, and modeling how authentic communication can transform conflict into connection. In both her writing and her living, Persinger shows us that crossing the bridge to understanding isn't just possible—it's transformational."

—Doug Lynam, author of *Taming Your Money Monster*

"This book is more than a set of instructions on communication skills. It is also the story of Trime Persinger's determination to confront and repair the trauma of relationship breakdown in her personal life. I highly recommend this important book to any reader seeking to bridge the divide when barriers go up in difficult times."

—Susan Gillis Chapman, author of
The Five Keys to Mindful Communication

"This insightful book is a wise and skillful guide to helpful and effective communication. Highly recommended."

—Gaylon Ferguson, author of *Welcoming Beginner's Mind*

CROSSING THE BRIDGE

Heal Your Relationships
with Courageous Communication

Trime Persinger

ENNEA DEEP LLC

Published by Ennea Deep LLC
Richland, Washington

Crossing the Bridge / Trime Persinger—1st edition

Edited by Sallamah Aliah

ISBN 979-8-9942230-0-0 (paperback)
ISBN 979-8-9942230-1-7 (eBook)

Library of Congress Control Number: 2026901800

Author website: TrimePersinger.com

For Ryan, Hayley,

Katarina, Tomika, and Flo

*"Man must evolve for all human conflict a method
which rejects revenge, aggression and retaliation.
The foundation of such a method is love."*

—The Reverend Dr. Martin Luther King Jr.

Contents

Foreword

From the moment I met Trime Persinger, I could tell this was a woman who consistently does her own inner work. There was a steadiness in her presence, a kind of grounded sincerity that made me feel both safe and seen. Trime is not interested in performance. She is devoted to the truth. And that devotion is precisely what makes her such a trustworthy guide in the delicate work of relationship repair.

This book, *Crossing the Bridge*, offers profound value. Not because communication is a trendy topic, but because communication is the heartbeat of every relationship we have, including the relationship we have with ourselves. We live in a time when many people are overwhelmed, reactive, and exhausted. We are living with stress, grief, uncertainty, and deep societal polarization. In that kind of climate, even the most loving relationships can become strained. Conversations can unravel quickly. Good intentions can be lost in moments of defensiveness, misunderstanding, or silence.

The beauty of Trime's work is that she does not shame us for our humanity. She meets us with compassion, then equips us with practical, accessible, and deeply transformative tools. This is not a book about learning the perfect script or mastering a technique. It is a book about developing the inner capacity to stay present, to speak clearly, and to listen with the kind of openness that creates connection rather than conflict.

One of the most powerful insights in these pages is the way Trime helps us understand the internal sequence that often shapes our communication. An event occurs, a story forms, emotions rise, and we act. That simple awareness can change everything. When we learn to recognize what is happening inside of us, we begin to regain choice. We can pause before we react. We can speak with clarity rather than from impulse.

We can become responsible for our feelings without projecting them onto someone else. And in doing so, we create the possibility for healing.

In my own work, I have witnessed that many of the conflicts we experience are not really about the topic at hand. They are about longing and feeling unseen. When our old wounds get activated, the survival strategies we developed long ago to protect ourselves are triggered. What makes this book so compelling is that it addresses communication not only as a relational skill but as a spiritual and emotional practice. It invites you to become more conscious, more compassionate, and more courageous. It invites you to return to your center, even when the moment feels hard.

Trime offers honest, deeply human stories, and she pairs them with a clear framework that helps you move from conflict to understanding. Her approach honors the complexity of relationships while still offering structure, guidance, and hope. You will find yourself learning how to speak, and also how to listen differently. Not only how to express your needs, but how to hold space for the experience of another. And perhaps most importantly, you will begin to trust that even difficult conversations can become a pathway to deeper intimacy when approached with intention.

If you are reading this book, you may be at a crossroads. You may be longing for repair in a relationship that matters to you. You may be tired of repeating patterns that leave you feeling disconnected. Or you may simply be ready to grow. Whatever brings you here, I want you to know this. Healing is possible. Connection is possible. And the bridge can be crossed.

This book will not ask you to become someone you are not. It will ask you to become more fully who you are, with greater awareness, greater tenderness, and greater integrity. That is the gift of Courageous Communication, and that is the gift Trime offers so beautifully in these pages.

May this book serve you.

May it strengthen your relationships.

And may it bring you back, again and again, to the love that is always waiting beneath the surface.

With gratitude,
Deborah Threadgill Egerton, Ph.D.

Preface

During my mom's second marriage, I was always scared to come home. Each day after school I would enter the house with trepidation and try to get a read on the situation. Was there fighting going on? Was my mom angry? Was my stepsister speaking to me? I needed to assess all these things so I could adjust my behavior accordingly. If there was discord, I would retreat as much as I could and try to stay out of the fray. If all was well, I could relax. Even then, any sense of peace could evaporate in an instant when someone said the wrong thing or looked the wrong way.

The evenings were the worst. My mom and stepfather drank a lot and fought a lot. One time late at night, my mom and my stepfather were yelling ferociously at each other in their bedroom. The sounds carried throughout our large home. The seven children of our blended family, ages six to seventeen, had already gone to bed but we had been awakened by our parents' enraged accusations and denials. We all lay frozen in our beds, listening and frightened, waiting for the fighting to end and hoping that my stepfather would not become violent.

Finally, I couldn't take it anymore. I got up and walked into the narrow corridor that led to their bedroom, hesitating as I sensed the danger zone ahead. To my left was a wall, to my right were closet doors painted pale yellow. Then I stepped into the room and begged them to stop. At that point the other kids got up and came into the bedroom too, everyone yelling at the same time. It was mayhem. In a fury, my stepfather smashed a framed picture of my grandmother and held a piece of the broken glass in his hand. I was terrified that he was going to stab my mom with the glass and kill her. I don't know whether I screamed outwardly or just inwardly, but the trauma of that moment is seared into my memory.

On other occasions when my mom and stepfather were fighting, a pair of uniformed police officers would show up at our front door. I never knew what prompted their arrival until I learned, much later, that our neighbors had called them out of concern for us. The police would settle things down and my mom would take my brother, my sister, and me to my grandparents' home. After a few days, my stepfather would show up there, sober and loving. Then she would take us back to his house until the next time.

Like most children, I thought that my family was normal. I internalized what I witnessed: that the way to deal with differences was to get defensive and blame others. I believed that other people were responsible for my anger, and that I was responsible for theirs.

More Terror

Time went by. I graduated from high school and college, then got married and moved to a small town, where my two children were born. When they were four and two, one day I loaded them into the back seat of our car to take them to day care. I had arranged to pick up a third child on the way. As my kids and I were sitting in the car outside the house waiting for the other child, there was an ear-splitting bang and a big convex dent popped up in the hood of the car, which had exploded under our feet. From the house, the child's mom yelled, "Get the kids out!"

I quickly rushed the children out of the car and we all stood a distance away, dazed. Fortunately, no one had been physically injured other than temporary ringing in the ears. I had the car towed to a car dealership, where the owner assured me that the explosion was not a malfunction of the car. "You need to call the police," he said. So I did.

It turned out that the explosion had been caused by dynamite wired to the exhaust pipe with a heat-sensitive fuse. Over the following year and a half, there were two more dynamite explosions targeting our car and our house, although it never happened again when the car was being driven. In addition, evidence clearly indicated two other unsuccessful attempts. While the property damage was substantial, fortunately no one was physically injured in any of the attacks. Despite extensive police investigations, we never learned who was attacking us, or why. After our ordeal hit the national news, the attacks stopped.

The impact on us, however, continued for years. Until we moved away from that house, my husband and I got out of bed several times each night and peered out our bedroom window to see if someone was approaching. We processed the events as best we could with our children, and each of us went through significant internal shifts. Together, we resolved not to let our lives be ruled by fear.

Searching for Answers

To this day, the source of the bombings remains a mystery. We considered moving away but knew that the unknown assailant could find a way to attack us wherever we went. I started looking at life more deeply, seeking comfort and guidance.

A few months after what turned out to be the final bombing, I found my way to Shambhala Buddhism. There I received teachings on fearlessness—allowing myself to feel fear, remain aware of it, and not succumb to it through acting out or shutting down. The teachings spoke directly to my life situation, and I dove in.

As part of my Buddhist path, I started practicing mindfulness meditation regularly. Meditation helped to settle my mind and gave me some insight into my fear and my other patterns of thinking.

Right before one meditation program, my husband confessed to me that he had engaged in a brief extramarital affair. I was devastated but attended the program anyway, practicing mindfulness as best I could in the midst of my inner turmoil. Then, on the third day of the program, I experienced an ongoing sensation of falling through space. I felt terrified and had a strong impulse to bolt from the room, but stayed because I knew that it would soon be my turn for a one-on-one session with the program instructor. I hoped that someone more experienced might be able to help me understand what I was going through, which would ease my panic.

When my turn came, I told the instructor about my sensation of falling and my fear, and asked her if this was the suffering I had heard about in Buddhism. She said, "No. It's warriorship." In Shambhala Buddhism, warriorship is another term for fearlessness. Upon hearing her words, I realized that I did not need to resist the sensation of falling. No matter how frightened I felt at this loss of control, I would be okay. Something inside me shifted and I instantly felt settled, open, and in touch with a larger reality.

For decades afterwards, Buddhism was my spiritual home.

My Next Step—Conflict Resolution

While meditation helped me to self-reflect and broadened my perspective, it did not give me tools for relating with other people or show me how to deal with my own anger. I still did not even know I had a problem. I was working as a realtor and thought I was doing okay. Then I took a half-day class in conflict resolution offered by my professional association. As I sat listening to the instructor, I felt surprised and intrigued. What was he talking about? There was a way to resolve conflicts? A way that did not involve winners and losers? A way you could study and learn?

After the class was over, I approached the instructor and asked him where he had learned all this. He gave me the name of a training program. I contacted them and requested their catalog, which listed page after page of courses teaching skills for resolving differences. With a mixture of excitement and apprehension, I signed up for their three-day introductory course.

In class, the instructor led us through concepts and exercises that were as unfamiliar to me as a foreign language. By the end of my first day of training I felt stunned and bewildered, as though the earth had shifted beneath my feet. I began to see how much I had to learn, and it shook me. I was scared of what lay ahead. But once the door had been opened, I knew there was no turning back.

On the second day of training we learned the skill of beginning sentences with the word "I." I had never heard of such a thing and felt alarmed. It seemed to me that beginning sentences with the word "I" would be egotistical, which would go against everything I had been learning in Buddhism. I also felt suspicious of my strong reaction since this secular wisdom seemed to be well established. I thought about it more and reasoned that if "I" Language did indeed promote my ego, I would recognize that and could stop using it. And maybe, just maybe, there was something there for me to learn. So I decided to try it anyway. (It turned out that "I" Language is not at all egotistical. Indeed, it was the doorway to a whole new understanding for me.)

I cautiously took more courses, scheduling them at long intervals so I had time in between to absorb the information. I was determined to give it my all, so I began to use the skills I was learning in my daily interactions with others. At first I felt awkward and embarrassed, like a small child in a grown-up world. I was afraid that people would mock me for sounding so strange.

Nevertheless, I persevered. To my surprise, no one mocked me. In fact, people opened to me as never before. My conversations became more interesting, and less about me. I learned things about people I thought I knew well. My constant sense of being on guard began to diminish.

Something else was happening too. Not only did I learn things about other people, I learned things about myself. Each time I intentionally used a skill, I overrode a habitual pattern that the skill was replacing. The contrast between the skill and the habitual pattern was so vivid, it brought that pattern into my awareness.

I began to see that my way of communicating had been keeping me trapped in a self-centered cocoon. Reluctantly, I started to realize that I had been using my speech to maintain control and to promote my own point of view, and that my communication had often conveyed judgment and a lack of personal responsibility. Oh, how it hurt to realize these things!

Using better communication skills also supported me in times of conflict, which was the intended purpose of the training. Previously, in conflict situations I would try to appease the other person or to dominate them, or else shut down. Meaningful dialogue never happened in the tense moments of my life; I had no idea it was even possible to have a constructive conversation at such times. Now I was learning skills I could use for that very purpose.

Along the way, I came to see that my predictable response to someone "pushing my buttons" meant that I had been giving away my power to anyone who could provoke or intimidate me. Even though I still felt uncomfortable, angry, or scared in such situations, I slowly realized that I could control my outward response. I would reach into my new communication toolbox and pull out some simple technique that might ease the situation—and it usually did.

I practiced and practiced. Eventually, the skills became my normal way of communicating, and my life became richer and more harmonious than it had ever been before.

Expanding Out with the Skills

Soon after I completed conflict-resolution training, I started teaching the skills I had learned. I developed a program that was rooted in the training I had received, enhanced with further reading and exploration, and presented in a way that reflected my deepening understanding of what the skills were really about. I presented this program to religious groups, schools, government agencies, and business groups. I also coached clients, published several articles online, and wrote the first draft of this book.

A few years later, I answered "the call" and became a prison chaplain, leading the prison's Buddhist program and doing the many other tasks entailed in prison chaplaincy. The communication skills I had learned enabled me to develop positive relationships with inmates and staff and to set boundaries as needed. Altogether, they made it possible for me to have a sixteen-year career that I loved.

As part of my chaplain role, I adapted my conflict-resolution training program to a prison context and taught it to inmates. In an environment fraught with hostility, deception, and fear, the skills helped people to build positive relationships and to resolve conflicts before they escalated. Inmates used these skills with family members and friends outside prison, with their fellow inmates, and even with staff. Time after time, they told me that learning the skills had changed their lives.

And now...

Having refined, tested, and taught these skills over decades, and having thought deeply about the world view they represent, I now offer you what I have learned and discovered. May this information support and assist you in your own journey toward a more authentic and loving life.

Introduction

*"Communication works for those
who work at it."*

—John Powell

Communication is a fundamental aspect of being human; it's how we convey information and connect with each other. But despite our ability to speak and hear words, sometimes we don't relate with each other as well as we would like. Our relationships can feel distant or disjointed. We might sense that there is a better way, and perhaps we have tried to make some changes. But in the face of challenges, we can end up repeating old patterns and feeling frustrated with other people (and perhaps with ourselves).

Courageous Communication is the art of holding the uncertain balance between yourself and another as you travel the journey of life together for a moment or for much longer. Courageous Communication differs from other approaches in that it provides a unique conceptual framework, it offers concrete, step-by-step instructions, and it addresses the very real difficulties we encounter when we try using the skills.

In the many books on communication that are available, there's a tendency to overlook how hard it is to actually change the way you communicate. The skills are universal, and it isn't that hard to understand them. You might even practice them in the context of a class or workshop. But applying them in a way that changes your life, and changes you—well, that's another thing entirely.

That's why I wrote this book. I learned these things myself, the hard way, and I want to show you how it can be done. I won't pretend it's easy to change your communication patterns—they are ingrained, like deep ruts in a muddy road. It takes effort to jump out of those ruts and create a new road on higher, firmer ground. I will offer suggestions and support and fresh ideas about how to do this, and lots of encouragement to be gentle with yourself. Nobody, not even me, gets it right all the time. Even still, it's worth the effort.

When people think about communicating better, they often think that it means learning different ways to speak. A central theme of this book, though, is that effective communication usually begins with listening to other people. You "cross the bridge" into their world to understand what they are trying to tell you. For most of us, this does not come naturally. *We* want to be heard, *we* want some attention! The point is, that is exactly what the other person wants too. And if you give it to them at the beginning of a conversation, they will be much more inclined to hear what you have to say later. Plus, you might learn something interesting and valuable.

Part I of the book, "Bridge Foundations," talks about three principles that underlie this approach to communication: the importance of human connection; the necessity of self-reflection as a doorway to everything else; and the connection, learning, and growth that can result from learning (and using) simple communication skills.

Part II is entitled "Why Is It So Difficult to Cross the Bridge?" Each chapter explores an aspect of human experience that makes it harder for us to connect with each other: our preferences, our certainty, and our anger. Then there is a chapter on the mechanics of conflict, including a discussion of where the choice points are.

This is followed by Part III, "Preparing to Cross the Bridge." The first chapter in this section gives instructions on how to learn the skills. The second chapter presents a key premise of Courageous Communication—that the best outcome of a difficult conversation is one that works for both you and the other person. Stating this intention is your fallback, what you can do when nothing else seems to be working.

Part IV, "Skills for Crossing the Bridge," begins with three chapters on various ways to listen. Yes, there is more than one way to listen! The skills range from silent listening, to repeating back, to hearing (and affirming) what *isn't* being said—the experience that lies beneath someone's words. Then there's a chapter on things to be careful about, and another chapter on asking questions.

Of course, communication is not just about crossing the bridge. It's also about giving voice to your own thoughts and feelings. So Part V is "Skills for Your Side of the Bridge." The essence of these skills is that you speak entirely *for yourself*, which means revealing your inner experience and staying away from any kind of blame. For many of us, including myself, this runs counter to lifetime habits. *And* adopting this approach enhances your power, your dignity, and your effectiveness. The three chapters in this section show you how to express yourself authentically, how to give negative feedback, and how to set personal boundaries.

The single chapter in Part VI, "The Bridge is Here and Now," talks about the importance of expanding your awareness and saying what you notice about the other person and yourself *in the present moment.*

Part VII, titled "Using the Bridge in Challenging Situations," includes a chapter laying out a strategy for difficult conversations and a chapter on what to do when someone is upset with you.

Part VIII, "Fruits of the Journey," includes chapters on autonomy, compassion, and presence—three qualities that emerge over time when you use the skills consistently, picking yourself up when you fall down and being as gentle with yourself as you can.

Many real-life stories are used to illustrate different principles or techniques. I collected these stories from clients and from people in my classes; some of them are my own. Each one really happened, although most names and some of the details have been changed. Stories that were told to me by others are indicated by a subheading with the person's name (or a pseudonym). My own stories are woven into the narrative or given a topical subheading.

There is so much to communicating! Each of us is beautifully unique and complicated, and there are endless ways we can arrange ourselves around each other. Sometimes we adjust to another person by following their lead, sometimes we move in sync with them, and sometimes we choose not to yield at all. It's like a dance between partners, with mutual give and take over time and endless permutations.

Courageous Communication includes skills for all these different ways of relating with another person, and suggestions for when to use each skill. You will learn *what* to do, *when* to do it, and *how* to do it. You will also learn about common traps and missteps, and you will receive support for continuing even when it's hard.

You might believe that this process requires the other people in your life to get on board with you and learn the skills too. While it's true that communication is a two-way street, I can assure you that it only takes one person—you—to change the dynamic of a conversation or a relationship. When you use the skills, other people tend to respond in kind. And if they don't, there are skills for expressing your dissatisfaction effectively and creating verbal boundaries.

The rewards of embarking on this adventure are immense. You will become more effective in connecting with others and in expressing your own perspective, even in tense moments. You will also discover more about who you truly are. The benefits are real and can happen quickly.

So let the journey begin!

Part I

Bridge Foundations

Chapter 1

Human Connection

"No man is an island."

—John Donne

When I was eight years old, my mom and dad got divorced and my mom was awarded full custody of my brother, my sister, and me. The following summer, she moved us from our home in Huntington, West Virginia to Victoria, British Columbia, where her parents had retired. Victoria was a long way from West Virginia and a long way from my dad.

My dad visited us in Victoria a few months after we moved. But after my mom remarried the next summer, he never came again, and we never went back to West Virginia. I wrote a few letters to him early on, and he might have written back. But then he stopped writing, and I gave up writing to him. Each month I would see a support check addressed to my mom in the mail—I recognized his handwriting on the envelope. It was a regular, painful reminder that he was out there somewhere and was aware that I existed. But there was never a letter for me, nor for my brother or sister, and never a long-distance call. Although my mom assured me that my dad loved me, I did not feel his love.

My dad's absence was an ever-present hole in my life. He seemed like a fantasy that was endlessly out of reach and I shed many, many tears of longing for him. The hole was filled for a time by my stepfather, but that relationship quickly became emotionally unsafe for me and eventually ended when my mom got divorced for a second time. Meanwhile, my longing for my dad continued.

I wrote to him again when I was seventeen, and he sent a warm reply. While I was overjoyed to receive his letter (and still have it), I did not write to him again. Looking back, I think I wanted him to initiate contact the next time. But he never did.

I did, however, stay in contact over the years with my paternal grandmother in West Virginia, "Mommay." Every birthday I would receive a card from her, check enclosed, as did my brother and sister, and she would always send my mom a check to buy Christmas gifts for us. I would send a thank-you note. She would reply, I would reply to her letter, and so we wrote back and forth.

When I was nineteen, I wrote to Mommay and asked her if I could come for a visit. She happily agreed and offered to buy me a plane ticket, which I accepted.

In those days people could meet passengers as they disembarked from the plane. When I descended the stairs from the plane onto the tarmac in Charleston, West Virginia, I saw two figures waiting in the dark. Somehow I knew that these two people belonged to me, that they were my family. One of them was a small woman, Mommay. For a moment I thought that the other person, a large man, was my dad. I caught my breath, I wanted to see him so badly. But when I got closer I realized that it wasn't my dad after all. It was an older man who turned out to be my grandfather's brother, Great-Uncle Meredith. My grandfather had died several years before.

Mommay took me to her home in Williamson, West Virginia, my birthplace. On most days of my two-week visit we were joined by her mother, Mom Strosnider, who was as round and soft as I remembered. I loved being with the two of them. It felt like an extended embrace, reminding me of a time when family made sense and all was right with the world.

Mommay introduced me to all her friends and re-acquainted me with some people I had known as a child. I asked her if I would get to see my dad, who still lived in Huntington. She tensed up and said, "No, that won't be possible." When she had called my dad to tell him that I was coming, he had become angry and had not spoken to her since. She did not know why, nor did she know what to do about it. He was her only child and had never cut her off like that before.

I could not believe that I had come all this way and still would not get to see my dad. I wept, and Mommay wept with me.

One day we made the three-hour drive to Huntington to visit Pat and Buddy, old friends of my parents and my brother's godparents. When Pat and Buddy heard about my dad's reaction to the news of my visit, they could not believe it. They were still close friends with him so Buddy called him at work. When he answered, Buddy told him that I was there in Huntington and asked him, didn't he want to see me? My dad told Buddy that it was none of his business and hung up. He reacted the same way to another of his close friends who called him on my behalf.

Throughout my visit, my dad had occupied my thoughts endlessly. Back at Mommay's home in Williamson, I was struck with a deep knowing: I must do everything in my power to see him before I left West Virginia. So I asked Mommay to drive me to his workplace in Huntington. I would present myself to him, face to face. Mommay said that she was worried about how he would receive me, or if he would see me at all. She did not want me to be hurt more than I already was. But I felt clear and strong, determined to make one last attempt. Reluctantly, Mommay said she would take me.

The next day we drove back to Huntington. We said very little as we drove along the mountain roads, each of us lost in our own thoughts. I had no idea what would happen when I showed up. I just knew that I needed to go. I felt scared but unwavering.

We drove up to my dad's workplace, a sprawling one-story industrial manufacturing plant. We agreed that Mommay would come back for me in one hour. I got out of the car and she drove away.

I walked from the curb to the building's entrance, opened the glass door, and went inside. I walked past a small seating area and up to the reception counter. I asked the receptionist, "Is John Persinger here?" There was a tall man standing behind her holding some papers—I had interrupted their conversation. The receptionist said, "Who shall I say is asking?" I said, "I'm his daughter."

The man looked at me strangely then said, "Follow me." I went through a door beside the reception counter then followed him down a narrow, well-lit corridor. Intuitively, I knew that he was my dad. I had no idea where he was taking me or what would happen when we got there. I felt like I was in free fall and was terrified. Nevertheless, I kept walking. This was what I had come for.

He led me into an office and closed the door, then pulled me to him and embraced me tightly as I cried harder than I had ever cried before. I howled as he held on. Eventually my tears subsided. Then we sat down and talked for the first time in ten years. As we sat there, I reached out and touched his knee several times saying, "I can't believe it's really you." My dad was no longer a fantasy to me. He was a real person, and I had found him at last.

In that conversation, I learned that Dad had been upset with me for arranging my trip to West Virginia with Mommay and not with him. That was why he had refused to see me until I presented myself to him in person. I also learned that his lack of contact with me over the years was because Mom had taken us so far away and then remarried. He felt cut off from his three children, just as we had felt cut off from him. When he and I finally reconnected that day in his office, each of us learned that the love between us had never diminished.

I now believe that Dad had not remotely fulfilled his parental responsibilities despite the monthly support payments, but at the time I did not care. Forgiveness came naturally and I simply celebrated our renewed connection.

From that point on, Dad and I communicated regularly. He came to know me, and I came to know him. He attended my wedding and was delighted to meet my firstborn, Ryan—his first grandchild.

Although Dad died a few years after Ryan was born, I still feel his presence in my life. Showing up at his workplace was one of the most courageous things I have ever done. Without doubt, it was also one of the most worthwhile.

It's All About Connection

Reconnecting with Dad was one step in the bumpy road of my life. Before and since, there is story after story of connections made, sustained, strained, repaired, and sometimes lost or broken. My connections with others, or their absence, are woven into the very fabric of my life's journey. It's the same for all of us.

Growing up without Dad in my life, and with a difficult home environment, I absorbed the lesson that connections were conditional and that I had to behave a certain way in order to be loved. Perhaps it would have been the same if he had been present, but it was certainly my experience without him there. I learned that mistakes were punished and resulted in disconnection. I adapted by trying hard to be good and by building a self-protective wall around myself because, deep down, I believed that I was fundamentally flawed and could never be "good enough" to be truly connected with others. While I longed for such connections, my behaviors and beliefs sabotaged the very connections I was seeking.

It was the communication skills in this book that changed everything. In every aspect of my life, they have enabled me to cultivate and strengthen the connections I always longed for. In a surprising way, the skills have also given me glimpses of my own inherent worthiness.

When I meet new people, I no longer worry about what I'm going to say. I just ask them about themselves and pay attention to what they tell me. Eventually, they usually ask me about myself and I'm able to talk without self-consciousness. When I'm feeling hurt or upset, I'm able to express myself without aggression. I'm also able to express compassion for others without needing to fix them.

My life keeps getting richer and more rewarding, and connections abound. Who knew that a few simple skills could make such a difference?

But they do.

Chapter 2

The Inner Journey

*"We are each a world, actually, a universe of
possibilities. To make effective change in the outer
world, we have to make effective change
in the inner world."*

—Ciela Wynter

For each of us, the journey of life includes the events and circumstances that impact us, as well as our internal way of making sense of it all. While we can't do anything about the things that happened in the past, we *can* be intentional about exploring our inner landscape. This is one way to learn and grow.

We all have our own way of looking inside. For me, Buddhist meditation has been a cornerstone. Early in my Buddhist training, I participated in a month-long group meditation retreat. The daily schedule included several hours of mindfulness meditation interspersed with walking meditation, work period, and meals. During the meditation sessions we sat on cushions in rows, all facing an altar at the front of the room. Our practice was to sit still with our eyes lowered and keep bringing our attention back to our breath.

When the gong sounded to initiate a period of walking meditation, we pushed the cushions together in the center of the room. Then we walked slowly in a circle around the stacked cushions, eyes lowered, placing our attention on our feet. When it was time to return to sitting meditation, we put the cushions back in rows and sat down. With another ringing of the gong, we returned to following the breath.

One day towards the end of the retreat, we had finished a period of walking meditation and were straightening the cushions. I had carefully placed the cushion in front of me in its correct location. The person whose cushion it was, though, had a different idea of where it should go. His name was Paul.

When Paul returned to his cushion after I had placed it, he glared at me and then moved it several inches to the left. The battle over his cushion placement had been building between us for several days, and he seemed to be throwing down the gauntlet. Then the gong sounded. We sat down and returned to sitting practice.

I felt frustrated and angry. Could Paul not see where his own cushion was supposed to go? Really, it was so obvious! But we were meditating, which meant that all I could do was sit there, my self-righteous anger punctuated by brief moments of paying attention to my breath. Gradually, my mind settled down and I began to appreciate the humor in the situation. If ever there was a tempest in a teapot, this was it.

On the way out of the meditation hall at the end of the session, Paul and I happened to walk beside each other. As we exited the room together, I looked at him, winked, and grinned. He smiled back, and the tension between us evaporated. We were friends.

For the first time in my life, I had spontaneously lightened up in the midst of a self-righteous rant. The long hours of meditation, day after day, had paid off in that moment of letting go. For once, I had made friends with my discomfort. Doing that changed the situation, and it changed me.

Over time, daily meditation practice has helped me to gain both personal insight and a larger perspective. It's always humbling, and sometimes refreshing, to think about life this way. I don't have to take myself so seriously, after all.

When you start experimenting with Courageous Communication, it will feel uncomfortable and sometimes just plain wrong—the way I felt about Paul's cushion. It will be your willingness to self-reflect, and override your habitual patterns, that will enable you to make the changes and reap the rewards.

Sandra

Sandra found her way with the help of a good therapist. In childhood, she experienced both societal violence and a traumatic home environment. Her dad was either enraged or depressed most of the time and sexually abused her from the time she was eight until she was thirteen. Her mom offered little comfort or protection. Sandra's dad died when she was fifteen, creating more confusion and grief. When she turned eighteen, she left home.

Sandra began drinking a lot, using drugs, and being promiscuous. In her early twenties, she started to see how unhappy she was. She explored alternative ways to ease her pain—twelve-step recovery, self-help books, and meditation retreats. Despite these efforts, her lifestyle didn't change. She knew a lot of people but didn't trust anyone and had no real friendships.

Then Sandra started seeing a therapist named Amy, who bore unflinching witness to Sandra's life story. Amy encouraged Sandra to reflect on her pain, including the ways in which she was continuing to perpetuate her own suffering. Sandra felt seen by Amy and loved by her. Over time, Amy helped Sandra to see the connection between her self-destructive behavior and her traumatic childhood. In each therapy session, Amy gave Sandra the message that she was worthwhile and that she was lovable.

Through Amy's compassionate, no-nonsense approach, day after day, week after week, year after year, Sandra began to see what Amy saw, to look inward with compassion for herself, and to take responsibility for her life.

One day Sandra woke up and realized that she had friends, people she could trust. Over the ensuing years her friendships have endured and deepened. She fell in love with a man whom she eventually married. She became an accomplished professional in her field.

Therapy helped Sandra to transform her life.

Be Like a Lion

You might not need meditation or therapy to self-reflect. Whatever your method, some form of self-reflection is essential for personal growth and change, including the change of learning Courageous Communication.

But it's easy, and more comfortable, to look at others! It's like throwing a stick for a dog, who eagerly chases after the stick—just as we are inclined to run after our thoughts and look outside ourselves for answers. If you throw a stick for a lion, though, you get a very different response. The lion's attention does not follow the stick. She looks back to see where the stick came from.[i]

Now, when I think of blaming someone, I try to be more like the lion and remember to look back toward the one who is throwing that stick of blame—myself. When I complain or fret or try to change others, I try to be curious about what's really going on for me underneath my irritation. Then I can be more effective at expressing myself and resolving differences.

Be Gentle with Yourself

I also had to give up blaming myself, or at least try. For many years, people who knew me well told me to stop being so hard on myself. I felt no connection with what they were saying, but I kept hearing the same thing so I figured there must be something to it. Gradually, I started recognizing the relentless pounding of my inner critic. But I still had no idea what to do about it.

One day, I was lying on my back on the floor having just completed a yoga routine. For the thousandth time, I wondered how I could lighten up on myself. An image came to me—Glinda, the Good Witch of the

North in the original version of *The Wizard of Oz*.[ii] In my mind's eye she hovered in the air a few feet above me, her radiant smile beaming down at me. She was dressed just like in the movie and held a wand in her right hand.

I imagined Glinda telling me that she loved me, with light emanating from her and surrounding me. Looking up at her I said, "Yeah, but I just did this terrible thing." I imagined her replying, "I don't care. I love you anyway." Then I thought of another terrible thing I had done and told her about it. She replied the same way, "I don't care. I love you anyway."

No matter how many terrible things I told Glinda I had done, her reply was always the same. In my mind, there was nothing I could do to make her stop loving me. It wasn't that she condoned my behavior. It was that whatever awful thing I had done did not diminish her love for me at all.

This flight of fancy allowed me to have a respite from my intense self-recrimination. Finally, I could relax for a moment. Finally, I could be okay being myself in the embrace of Glinda's unconditional love. That was how I started understanding what it means to be gentle with myself.

Without gentleness towards myself, my journey grinds to a halt. My guilt keeps me locked in the same groove, wishing I were different yet feeling helpless to change. Gentleness keeps me connected with my sad and tender heart[iii] as I lean into the full experience of my life. With gentleness, my challenges become opportunities for growth. Gentleness humbles me, liberates me from my addiction to myself, and enables me to carry on.

Including Others

When I was a young mother, I lived in a small town where everyone knew everyone else. One of the community leaders was an older woman named Kay. I felt a small amount of tension around Kay—for some reason, she pushed my buttons.

One day I was talking with Kay outside the local post office. The conversation was congenial, but I was aware of my resistance to her and my internal criticism of her. Then, spontaneously, it seemed as though a veil lifted and she came into focus for me as a fellow human being. My thoughts about her vanished and I saw *her*.

Including other people in my inner journey means making an effort to see them in this way. Recognizing that they matter, and that they are whole human beings with lives and stories of their own, requires me to step beyond my focus on myself. Working with my inner demons is important, but it is incomplete. My mind and my heart both expand when I extend my awareness to include others.

It takes effort to do this. When I find myself inwardly judging another person, I have trained myself to say silently, "May you be happy" or "You belong." This self-talk is an internal recalibration, a way to settle down inside my own skin and mentally allow them to be in theirs.

Without doubt, then, other people are part of my inner practice too. This is especially true for people who are in my life on an ongoing basis. With these folks, sometimes it's hard to cross the bridge! And sometimes it's hard to ask for what I want or express negativity. At the same time, being able to do these things is an essential component of the life I want to live. So when things aren't going my way I look inside, recalibrate, and figure out a way to move forward anyway. Sometimes I'm clumsy with my words, and it doesn't always go the way I planned. But even if I'm clumsy, usually some small opening appears and the situation starts to shift.

If I never looked inside at such times, I would fall into the trap of judgment and blame and would have no power at all.

Endless Learning

In the early years of my inner journey, when I read something especially helpful or profound I would think to myself, "Mom should read this." Eventually I came to realize that this thought was a clever way for me to resist my own need to learn. So when I caught myself thinking that "Mom should read this," I replaced it with "*I* should read this and take it to heart."

This practice of looking at myself continues in different ways. When I notice that I'm upset or stressed or tense for any reason, I consider it a signal to look inside and "do my own work." My entire life then becomes a path of discovery. In addition to my personal study and self-reflection, my inner journey includes all my relationships as well as my daily interactions with others. Nothing is excluded; I welcome it all. There is joy in this for me, and further surrender.

Surrendering in this way does not come easily to me—my patterns of thinking and relating run deep. My inner work, done with gentleness, slowly chips away at these patterns and enables me to show up for myself and others. My inner work forms the foundation of my life, to which I return again and again for insight and renewal. In the midst of my confusion, anger, and fear, I am reminded of a larger view and a greater understanding.

There is no end to this process; I never "arrive." The journey itself is what opens me up, enables me to grow, and connects me with others.

It's worth the effort.

Chapter 3

The Path of Words

"All growth entails discomfort."

—Russ Hudson

As a young man, Freddie used cocaine, marijuana, PCP, and alcohol, and relied on his fists to make his way in the world. His uncle, a Sunni Muslim, gave Freddie a Hadith[1] to help him get out of his "gutter thinking" and, hopefully, turn his life around. Freddie read the Hadith and started performing salat.[2]

But nothing else changed. After robbing a bank, Freddie was sent to federal prison for thirteen years. Inside the prison were inmate "families," of which the biggest was the family of Sunni Muslims. Freddie joined this group. He re-read the Hadith and his thought patterns started changing. He began performing salat again and re-established his good intentions.

After he was released from prison, though, Freddie went back to using his fists. A big fight landed him in state prison for ten years. While

---

[1] A record of the words, actions, and silent approvals of the Islamic prophet Muhammad as transmitted through chains of narrators (source: Wikipedia)

[2] The five daily prayers of Islam

he was there, he "got into his feelings" and assaulted a correctional officer, which earned him another seven years of incarceration.

During one long stint in the Intensive Management Unit (IMU), where he had been placed for fighting, Freddie was offered a training program in communication skills. Islam teaches its adherents to seek knowledge from all ends of the earth, so he decided to take the class. For this class, Freddie and his two classmates (all from IMU) sat in individual side-by-side steel cages in a small room. The instructor sat outside the row of cages facing the three of them. That instructor was me.

As a prison chaplain, I had developed a training program called *The Art of Communication*. In that small room, week by week, I led the three men through the curriculum. I taught them that all behavior makes sense to the person who is doing it and that other peoples' perspectives were as valid as their own. They learned listening skills and they learned how to respectfully give feedback. I also had them memorize a short statement to use when they found themselves in tense situations. They practiced all the skills with each other in exercises and role plays.

Freddie started using the skills right away. And his life changed, finally and permanently. After he was released from solitary confinement, he continued using the skills and gradually earned the respect of prison staff and inmates. Over the next several years he was given prison jobs with increasing responsibility. As a General Population inmate, he took The Art of Communication three more times and never used his fists again. When he was finally released from prison, he landed on his feet and started working immediately. He has never looked back.

Freddie says, "The tools in Islam and the tools of communication complement each other. If you use these tools, you can get out of any situation that you're in. But you have to seek and apply this knowledge. It doesn't just come to you. The Art of Communication gave me a whole new toolbox."

Freddie's story is not unique—the course benefited inmates from a wide variety of backgrounds. In my experience, these skills complement and deepen any spiritual practice or life journey. If you do this work, you will grow.

Getting Hooked

Like Freddie, and like all of us, I experience uncomfortable internal reactions to many circumstances and events—I get "triggered." This reaction is strongest for me when I'm feeling personally attacked. But even if there is a change in plans, or if I feel put on the spot, or if I perceive judgment from someone I respect, I often feel uncomfortable.

In the past, I did not recognize this discomfort. Instead, I attended to "the problem," which always seemed to be outside of me, by having some kind of knee-jerk reaction. I might verbally snap at someone, criticize them, or freeze up. Reactive behaviors such as these were as normal to me as breathing. Although my intention was to fix the problem or to make it go away, that seldom happened. Almost always, my reactive behavior made things worse for myself or for the other person. Usually for both.

To be honest, I'm still discovering ways in which I can be triggered. It happens inside me and is beyond my conscious control. But when an inner trigger leads to an outward, knee-jerk reaction, I've gotten "hooked."[iv] And even when I'm triggered, I can prevent myself from getting hooked. This is where Courageous Communication comes in.

Inserting a Pause

The following quote has been attributed to Viktor Frankl, Holocaust survivor and author of *Man's Search for Meaning*[v]: "Between stimulus and response there is a space. In that space is our power to choose our response. In our response lies our growth and our freedom."[vi]

Until I started using communication skills, the space between stimulus and response eluded me. Training myself to use these skills helped me to understand that I had a choice about how I reacted, and I was able to insert a pause more and more frequently. That freed me from being so strongly identified with the automatic reactions that had ruled my life.

Inserting a pause allows me to respond intentionally rather than react automatically. After I pause, I pull a tool out of my communication toolbox and proceed from there. Inside, I might still be stressed and uncomfortable. But I'm not making things worse for myself or for others.

When my internal reaction is intense, and if the situation allows, my "pause" can last a long time. It can take hours, days, or even weeks for me to be ready to address the issue—I force myself to wait until my emotional reaction has subsided and I can think more clearly. As the emotional intensity subsides, I start considering what I want to say. Authentic, well-timed communication has enabled me to move through some major difficulties, helping my relationships to deepen and grow.

In some situations, I don't have the opportunity to take a longer pause. But I can always try to recognize when I'm triggered, hit the pause button (however briefly), and shift gears. In situations like that, my training in communication skills can be the plank that saves me from drowning in the ocean of my panic or rage.

To this day, though, I can still lose myself in a strong reaction— especially self-righteous indignation. That feeling is so compelling for me! Being triggered in this way can lead me to act without thinking. When I cool down and realize that I've been hooked again, I practice being gentle with myself. Then, sooner or later, I get back in the saddle and keep going (which usually involves an apology).

Communication as Inner Work

Training myself to communicate differently when I'm triggered did not come easily. I gradually learned how to do this by practicing the skills in everyday conversations. I was training my brain so that these skills would be available to me in more stressful situations.

That's how I discovered the transformative potential of communication skills. Each time I used a skill, I shifted away from my habitual way of communicating. Doing this made me feel uncomfortable because it was new and unfamiliar. I felt exposed.

As I looked more closely at the discomfort I felt when I was trying to communicate differently, I saw that it was rooted in fear. What was I afraid of? I slowly came to see that I feared many things. I feared losing ground or shifting to accommodate another person's point of view. I feared change of any kind, for my sense of safety was founded on familiarity and control.

When I saw my fear for what it was, its grip on me loosened and I realized that I had a choice. I could continue to communicate the old way, which gave me the illusion of safety, or I could embark on this new, daring adventure of stepping more fully into my life by using the skills regardless of my emotional state. I chose the latter.

In the process of changing the way I communicated, I became less defensive and more curious about everything. I learned to appreciate the richness and complexity of my fellow human beings, and to deepen my understanding of myself. Using the skills over many years has enabled me to become softer, stronger, happier, and more resilient, and to discover the give and take of good human relationships.

Courageous Communication

To face my discomfort, to look beyond my own point of view, to try to see things as the other person does, to admit the possibility of being wrong—it all takes courage. It also takes courage to be true to myself without judging or blaming people.

This is not a panacea. Even in its purest form, Courageous Communication will not put an end to conflict or emotional discomfort in your life. But its consistent application will result in more meaningful relationships, greater depth of experience, and a broader, more compassionate view of yourself and the world.

If I can do it, and Freddie can do it, then you can do it too.

Part II

Why Is It So Difficult to Cross the Bridge?

Chapter 4

Preferences

"The world would be a vastly safer place—and maybe
a happier one, too—if more of us learned to see
beyond our biases, our preferences, and became
optimists capable of letting go."

—Thomas Chatterton Williams

A fundamental challenge to getting along well with others is the fact that each of us has personal preferences—we like some things better than others. When our preferences don't line up with the preferences of the other people in our lives, that can cause friction.

In my mind, the word "preference" used to apply only to mundane things such as flavors of ice cream. For things that were important to me, I believed that there was right and wrong, period. I could not imagine that my convictions, which seemed self-evident to me, were more about my personal preferences than about universal truths. Learning that my convictions were neither obvious nor universal, and that reality is more nuanced and interesting, was a long, painful process.

One of my central convictions used to be that people should "follow the rules." For the first part of my life, I had no tolerance for anything else. It seemed clear to me that following the rules made one a good person, and that breaking the rules was bad. When the rules were breached, my tendency was to blame the person I held responsible. Family members, friends, people in authority—no one escaped my accusing mind. I did not understand that the rules I adhered to so strongly were often *my* rules, and not necessarily theirs.

I felt tense and unhappy and did not know why. My standards often got in the way of my relationships with friends, colleagues, and family members. I believed that if only they would do what I thought they were supposed to do, then all would be fine. When I corrected them, I thought I was doing them a favor. When they told me to lighten up, I felt confused and irritated. I did not understand how anyone could possibly disagree with me. "They just don't get it," I thought. It never, ever occurred to me to cross the bridge.

As I had begun to learn through meditation practice, I needed to take myself less seriously.

Seeing Beyond Our Preferences

In the past, when my preferences were not being met I saw it as a problem outside myself that had to be solved. I truly believed that I was the one to solve it, and that people who thought differently than me were misguided or stubborn or foolish. It took me a long time to learn that no matter how strongly I believed something, that did not mean it was universally true.

When I mustered my courage and started using communication skills, really listening to other people, I began to realize that my way was not the only way. With this insight, I felt embarrassed and humbled. How could this be? And yet, I knew it was so. With this small glimpse of awareness, I started to relax and to shed the burden of being the world's savior. I also began the process of seeing my preferences for what they were—preferences only, not edicts. As this understanding gradually deepened in me, my preferences stopped controlling my life.

All Behavior Makes Sense

Just as my speech and behavior are expressions of my beliefs, perspectives, and preferences, so, too, the speech and behavior of others express *their* beliefs, perspectives, and preferences. And their beliefs are as real to them as my beliefs are to me. When people say or do things, their words or actions arise from their perspective at that moment. Whatever they are saying or doing makes complete sense to them.

The first time I heard this observation, it shocked me. What? All behavior makes sense? Other people have their own thoughts, feelings, motivation, and perspective? But as soon as I heard it, I knew it was true. Of course! How could it be otherwise?

Since learning this, remembering that "all behavior makes sense" has helped me through difficult situations countless times. When someone says something that doesn't make sense to me, I try to remember that it makes sense to *them*. The next step, then, is for me to get curious.

I can tell you with great confidence that curiosity works a thousand times better than confrontation to heal relationships and resolve conflicts.

A Larger View

Acknowledging the possibility that my personal view may not work for someone else marked a significant shift in the way I thought about everything. With halting steps, and many regressions, I began to expand my awareness to include a broader perspective. The discomfort that I felt when my preferences were not being met became an object of curiosity rather than a catalyst for self-righteous declarations. In this way, the preferences that I had held so dearly, and which had been the source of so much conflict, became opportunities for growth and learning.

I need not change my mind about issues that are important to me. I need only acknowledge that my answer may not be the answer for everyone. I could recognize that tolerance, compassion, and humor are more helpful to my relationships, and to me, than judgments. When I cross the bridge and remain curious in the presence of alternative points of view, I step beyond my zone of comfort into the realm of the unknown and endeavor to "…love the questions themselves as if they were locked rooms or books written in a very foreign language."[vii]

When I consider this larger view, I see that my preferences need not stand between myself and others. Indeed, holding my preferences within a greater context fosters insight, humility, and compassion, which in turn lead to greater understanding and connection. This is what I gain when I give up needing to be right.

Certainty

"Don't believe everything you think."

—Joseph Nguyen

I used to be certain about my preferences, my convictions, and everything else. Now I'm uncertain about most things, and my life is richer for it. My principles of honesty, fairness, and kindness have not changed. And I still have opinions about many things. But I hold it all much more lightly. I don't want my convictions, or my opinions, to create unintentional barriers with others.

Certainty can begin with our built-in need to understand our world. When something seems amiss, we are inclined to seek an explanation for it. For example, suppose that the yard of someone who lives down the street from you becomes overgrown. If you don't already know the reason for the lawn's condition, and you don't know them well enough to check in with them, ideas will start coming to you. You might assume that they are being lazy or irresponsible. Or you might assume that they are ill, or on vacation. Regardless, we always seem to need *some* explanation for what we see. If we don't already know, we tell ourselves a story. At the very least, we wonder about one.

The problem is not that we make up stories—that is a natural, ongoing human activity and an essential aspect of the creative process. When we believe our stories to be true, though, certainty has entered the picture. And our certainty can blind us. The more certain we are about something, the less inclined we are to consider other possible explanations.

The Fundamental Attribution Error

Attribution Theory explains the difference between how people understand their own behavior and how they understand the comparable behavior of other people. If we perceive someone else having difficulties, we can tend to attribute their behavior to an internal factor, such as a character flaw. On the other hand, our own difficulties seem to be due to external factors beyond our control. For example, if someone is late for an appointment, I might tell myself that they do not manage their time well. If I am the one who is running late, I might tell myself that it is because the traffic was heavy or I was attending to something important.

The opposite can be true for pleasant experiences. If I receive recognition for a job well done, I might be inclined to believe that my success is due to my personal effort and competence. If someone else receives recognition, I might believe it was because they knew the right people or they had good help.

The fact that we have different explanations for the same behavior is called the Fundamental Attribution Error.[viii]

In my experience, the Fundamental Attribution Error occurs more frequently, and with greater intensity, when we are in conflict with someone. If I've been having issues with the neighbor whose lawn is overgrown, I am more likely to judge them harshly for not mowing their grass. If my lawn is overgrown, I have a million reasons to explain it.

In general, it's easy for me to see myself as "the good guy" and the person on the other side of a conflict as "the bad guy." If I hold to that view with certainty, things invariably go from bad to worse.

Certainty Limits Us

As we all know, you can be certain and be wrong.[3] Once I disagreed with my grandfather about the definition of a word. To resolve the dispute, I referred to a dictionary. When Gramps saw that the dictionary definition of the word was the one I had given, he said that the dictionary was wrong.

Many times I have been as certain as my grandfather was, only to discover that I was wrong. Certainty clouds my vision, impedes my awareness of nuance and complexity, and impels me to judge others as either friend or foe—someone who agrees with me or someone who does not. Certainty is perhaps the greatest barrier to healing relationships or working effectively with conflict. When we are certain, we are not inclined to cross the bridge.

Even knowing this, it can be difficult to allow uncertainty into my world view when it's something I really care about. When I am confronted with a reality that does not conform with my view, I can feel embarrassed or even humiliated. The more certain I am, the more difficult it is to receive information that contradicts my belief or to hear someone else's perspective. So I work at being less certain about things.

While uncertainty can be painful and humbling, it also brings many rewards. It is gentler and more open. When I allow myself to be uncertain, I engage with other people in a more sincere, inquisitive, and heartfelt manner. I open to the world as it is, rather than as I *think* it is. There is a softening, a letting go. If I am in a conflict with someone and they are unwilling to budge, experience has shown me that uncertainty and curiosity will reach them far more effectively than my insistence that they are wrong. Curiosity strengthens my connection with them, rather than straining it.

Taking Things Personally

One way that certainty can cause problems for me is my tendency to

---

[3] For a wonderful discourse on the subject of being wrong, see *Being Wrong* by Kathryn Schulz (HarperCollins Publishers, 2010)

take things personally, believing that others are being critical of me. When I am caught in this mindset, even an off-hand remark can feel like a major attack. I find it difficult to imagine that the person's words might not be meant as some kind of judgment.

Finding my way in a new job, I experienced this repeatedly. It seemed that my supervisor was slighting me in various ways, and I felt uncomfortable. When I cautiously checked it out with her, I learned that her actions were motivated by other factors and had nothing to do with my behavior. Our relationship evolved over time as we learned more about one another. The two of us gradually came to trust each other and to appreciate the different strengths that each of us brought to the work-place. What a relief that was!

The closer I am to another person, the more likely I am to feel personally attacked by their comments. But I've been growing in this area. Now, when I am feeling judged or hurt by someone, I try to be less certain. I remember that all behavior makes sense and that what I heard as criticism might not have been intended that way at all. Eventually, I might check out my story with the other person, as I did with my supervisor. All this has helped me to free myself from believing that everything that happens is about me.[ix]

Roger

Roger was a first-time counselor at a summer camp for teenagers. Max, one of the youths at the camp, was a large, intense boy who often seemed to be scowling. Other counselors told Roger that he needed to have clear expectations and set boundaries with Max. Otherwise, Max would "walk all over him." Truly, Roger felt uncomfortable whenever Max was around.

There were over a hundred youths at the camp, and Roger was able to avoid Max for several days. But that did not feel comfortable for Roger, either. So one day he decided that he wanted to get to know Max better. He pulled Max aside, sat down with him, and said, "Max, you scare me." Max's eyes welled up with tears. He said he knew that he scared people and he didn't want to. Roger and Max talked for a while longer, getting to know each other. For the remainder of the camp, Max was openly respectful towards Roger and Roger no longer feared him.

Be Curious!

As Roger's conversation with Max shows, a willingness to question assumptions can lead to shifts in perception and greater insight. For this reason, *allow new information to influence you.* If you hear something that does not fit with your inner narrative, allow yourself to be surprised. Even in the heat of battle, you might hear something that you did not know before. When you create space for that new information, it can profoundly change the way you see the situation and how you feel about it.

Becoming less certain alters the tone of a conflict. It need not take much of a shift. By allowing even a little uncertainty, by being slightly curious, you create the possibility of a gap, of movement, of engaging more effectively with the other person.

Elie Wiesel, a Holocaust survivor and Nobel laureate, tells us that "Questions unite people. Answers divide them."[x] The more we rouse our curiosity and rest in uncertainty, the more we appreciate, even celebrate, the quirks and flaws that make each of us human. Uncertainty preserves our connections with the other people in our lives, and it opens the door to understanding.

Chapter 6

Anger

*"The goal isn't to never feel angry. The goal is to
understand your anger and to choose healthy ways
to respond to it."*

—Leticia Rae

In addition to the angry outbursts I frequently witnessed between my mom and stepfather, often I was the one on the receiving end of my mom's anger. She criticized my actions daily and often yelled at me. She punished me for my own expressions of anger, so there were two clear messages: it was okay for her to be angry with me, but it was not okay, or safe, for me to be angry with her. I desperately wanted my mom's approval, so I learned to suppress and disown my anger entirely. I also internalized her criticism of me, and believed that if I could only be good enough (perfect), then she would not be mad at me.

The family life I created with my husband was more stable than the one I had grown up in, but still I would sometimes erupt in rage. I would get frustrated with the children, reach a boiling point, and let loose. I remember one angry moment, a voice inside my head telling me not to yell and yelling anyway. Just like the anger I had been subjected to as a child, my own outbursts always included blame. I know that all parents get angry with their children at times. I'm talking about myself here, though, and I always regretted it afterwards. And yet, in my mind, I was not an angry person.

The bombings that occurred when my children were small were terrifying reminders of the parental anger I had experienced as a child, and I reacted as I almost always had reacted then—I froze. Even though our lives were truly at risk, I was not aware of any anger I felt in response to the threat. Instead, I tried to be "good" by consciously cultivating compassion for our assailants, whoever they were.

Even after I began to practice meditation regularly, I remained unaware of my anger. But my daughter Hayley remembers that after I began meditating, I did not get mad at her as much. Meditation, then, was a step in the right direction.

I spent the next decade continuing to believe that anger was not an issue for me. How blind I was! There were signs, but I ignored them. My husband and I had started a business and one of our employees quit her job because of me. With her and with everyone else, I needed things to be perfect (my version) all the time. My husband started telling me that he was afraid of my anger. A close friend said that my need for control was a form of anger. Although I was certain that I kept my voice even, Hayley would sometimes say that I was yelling at her.

These warnings made brief inroads into my self-righteousness, but overall my conscious reality was this: I was not angry. I knew that I was demanding but I also knew that I was right. The irritation I felt always seemed justified by the circumstances. It was everyone else who needed to change.

Moments of Truth

Then I started taking conflict-resolution courses. By the end of the first three-day course I had learned enough to know that my habitual responses were not serving me well, but I couldn't remember the new tools. During the final role play, I simply could not speak. At the end of the role play the instructor said, with great kindness, "Trime, you could inflate to your full size." I had no idea what she meant, but her words impacted me deeply. It has taken me a long time to begin to fulfill their promise.

As I continued with my training, eventually I found myself in a course called "Asserting Yourself Under Pressure." By this time I had acquired a certain level of skill. As a result, I was both more confident and more open. And then my world was rocked again. In response to one of my many questions, the instructor looked straight at me and said, "Your feelings are valid, and they are nobody's fault."

That one sentence hit me like a clap of thunder. How could this be? And yet, I knew she was right. My whole life, I had been blaming other people. Taking away blame stripped me of a fundamental frame of reference. Without this frame of reference, which focused my attention outward, I knew I had to look at myself. Instantly, viscerally, I came face to face with my anger.

Saying that my anger is valid means that it is a feeling like any other, with a life of its own. When I feel angry, that's my experience. My anger is neither good nor bad; it just *is*.

Saying that my anger is nobody's fault is an extension of this. My anger exists on its own, *independent of its external causes*. When I believe that my anger is someone else's fault, I make it about them instead of about me and so give away my power. My anger is mine and mine alone. To this day, I am amazed at the profundity of this life-changing insight.

Recognizing my Anger

My anger is triggered by thinking that something or someone in my world needs to be different than they are. Thinking that *I* need to be different is also an expression of my anger—anger turned inwards. It perpetuates my belief that there is something wrong with me, which fuels my self-directed anger further. There's no end to that kind of thinking. Anger is a natural part of my psyche, called forth from external situations or from deep within me. It's a survival mechanism that is there to protect me from real or perceived threats.

To claim my anger, I first have to recognize that it's present. I have found that anger shows up as tension in my body or harshness in my voice. There is also a narrowing of focus, a subtle sense of "me against the world." It's like I'm bracing myself for battle.

Here's the thing: there's nothing wrong with feeling angry. Whatever form my anger takes, and whatever its focus, I can choose to recognize it and take responsibility for it. This means allowing myself to feel what I feel and not make it about someone else. Doing this has become an integral part of my inner journey—another example of the lion and the stick.

Befriending Anger

When I realize that I'm feeling angry, I use one of the strategies I've developed to help me befriend my anger and gain a larger perspective. If I'm with someone I might say, "I'm feeling bristly." If I feel safe enough in that moment, I might even ask for a hug. When I'm by myself, sometimes I imagine the hug.

I might visualize Glinda, or my father, smiling down at me. I imagine them seeing me, seeing my anger, and loving me anyway. They let me know that it's okay for me to be myself as I am at that moment.

I might think of myself as a small child, feeling helpless and enraged. I see myself as both the parent and the child, and in my mind I hold my little girl as she lets herself feel what she's feeling in the safe embrace of my love.

I might notice the physical sensations that happen when I'm feeling angry—tight neck and shoulders, a lump in my throat. Then I say to that part of my body, "You're fine just as you are. You belong. I know you're trying to protect me. I'm here with you and we've got this." The sensations might not go away, but I stop fighting against them. I'm no longer trying to fix them or myself, and that helps them to subside over time. Or not. Either way, they are in my awareness and are no longer running the show.

It also helps me to alternate awareness of the places in my body that are holding tension, with awareness of other places that are more relaxed. Those other places, like my feet, are doing just fine. They can be resources for me, reminding me that there's more to me than my anger.

It's not only the anger and the physical sensations that belong. Sometimes I remind myself that *I* belong, just as I am, including the anger. The word "belong" has power for me, and reminding myself that I belong soothes me.

Whatever strategy I use, when I befriend my anger as best I can while loving myself at the same time, I always find an underlying experience of sadness. I comfort myself in the midst of that, too, using the same strategies.

The point is, I don't have to get rid of my anger, which is good because I can't. But I also don't have to let it rule my life. The only way I know how to loosen its grip is to bring it into the open, befriend it, and find ways to love myself anyway. Then I no longer need to blame myself or anyone else.

At the same time, when I'm angry with someone then my anger is pointing to a problem. Whether the problem is real or perceived, sooner or later I might decide to address it with them. Suggestions for doing this will be presented in "Skills for Your Side of the Bridge."

An Anger Story

I am hosting a meeting of a volunteer service group in my home. One member of the group, Carlos, has been edgy ever since he arrived. For the past week, Carlos and I have differed on a number of issues and our relationship has been strained. I have tried to communicate well, doing lots of listening and speaking with care. Internally, I have done my best to be gentle with myself and with Carlos. But the conflict has worn me down. I have been feeling weary and depressed and have resolved to assert myself more strongly in the relationship.

During the meeting, Carlos and I have very different perspectives on the direction that our group should take. After a few minutes of discussion, Carlos accuses me of promoting conflict between the two of us. In times past, at this point I would have either frozen or apologized or made a counterattack. Instead, I look him in the eye and say in a steady voice, "Back off with the accusations, Carlos." The discussion continues but soon afterwards, Carlos angrily announces that he is quitting the group. He gets up and leaves the meeting.

A few hours later, Carlos sends an e-mail to the group apologizing for his outburst, although he does not re-join us. I send an appreciative response. Despite this email exchange, memories of the conflict haunt me for days. I feel angry and sad and fearful of any contact with Carlos. I practice being gentle with each feeling as it emerges and recedes. Sometimes I cry. I contemplate my shared journey with Carlos, knowing that we are teachers for each other. I reflect on my own words in the conversation and know that I could have been more skillful. I also acknowledge that the moment when I stood up for myself, simply and directly, was a clean, healthy expression of my anger and a personal victory.

None of this is easy. I believe that Carlos, too, is haunted by what happened between us. He reaches out to me in a variety of ways over the ensuing weeks and, cautiously, I reach back to him. Slowly we re-build our friendship. Each setback—and there are many—shows me where I am hurting. I bear witness to my own pain, and to his. I contemplate how to protect myself without falling into self-righteousness, and how to cultivate compassion for both of us in the midst of it all. My practice is to see this journey with Carlos as an opportunity for healing, growth, and love.

I have come to understand that my way forward is to know my anger, even embrace it. By opening to the intensity of this emotion, despite my resistance, I also open to my sad and tender heart. In the process, I claim my power. I claim it with love for myself, for those I have harmed, and for all others whose anger masks their pain.

Sometimes, I feel angry. Sometimes, I feel angry.

Nevertheless, I will dance.[xi]

Chapter 7

Conflict

"Conflict can and should be handled constructively;
when it is, relationships benefit."

—Harriet Lerner

Despite our best efforts, the challenges discussed in the previous three chapters—our preferences, our certainty, and our anger—can lead to conflict. Perhaps it seems to us that we have done nothing to bring it on, but somehow a conflict presents itself. Whatever its origin, conflict is characterized by unresolved tension and a sense of disconnection between you and someone else.[4] Conflict feels like "you against me."

I used to feel helpless in conflict situations, at the mercy of my own feelings and the actions of the other person. No longer. While I still can't control what other people say or do, I now know that I can control myself. I can make different choices that can significantly alter the tone of the conversation, and its outcome, for the better.

This chapter presents a model that describes our inner process and shows us where we can make those different choices. Subsequent chapters discuss what our different choices might be.

---

[4] This discussion of conflict is about verbal conflict between two people. Situations of physical violence are not addressed.

How Conflict Happens

Our experience of interpersonal conflict follows a pattern. Although this pattern is familiar to us, it can be helpful to take a close look and examine its component parts.

First, something happens. I call this the *event*. Then a *feeling* arises. Then we *react*. I will illustrate this using an imaginary conflict situation.

Suppose that you have a close friend named Chris. You trust Chris and have recently shared sensitive information with him. A few days later a mutual friend, Morgan, tells you that she and Chris were discussing your sensitive information. Instantly, you assume that Chris betrayed your trust. You get triggered and react in some way.

Let's look at this scenario in more detail:

The Event

In this situation, the event is Morgan telling you that she and Chris were discussing your sensitive information. Morgan's disclosure is the catalyst that sets everything else in motion.

The Feeling

In the definition above, conflict is characterized by "unresolved tension and a sense of disconnection." By this definition, conflict *always* involves a feeling of some kind. In addition to tension and a sense of disconnection, you might also feel anger, fear, shame, or any number of other feelings.

It might be hard to recognize your feelings when difficult situations arise. Indeed, you might just feel numb (which is also a feeling). Nevertheless, by the definition I'm using, if you are in conflict with another person then you have feelings about it. If you feel calm, centered, and caring, then for you it's not a conflict.

The Reaction

There are different ways in which you might react automatically when Morgan tells you about her conversation with Chris:

Attack: You become irate over Chris's disclosure and tell Morgan that it is none of her business. Then you call or text Chris to express your rage. You might even start saying negative things about him to others.

Avoid: In your conversation with Morgan, you deny everything. With Chris, you pretend that it never happened. You are overly nice to him, but underneath you are boiling. You start finding ways to avoid him. When Chris finally asks you what is going on, you say, "Nothing." But you cannot get over your feeling of betrayal.

Self-blame: With Morgan, you stumble around and leave the conversation as quickly as possible. You withdraw from Chris. You blame yourself for your poor judgment in saying more to Chris than you should have. You have no idea how to make it better.

Any one of these automatic reactions does not preclude another—you might go through some combination of them over time. You might also have a particular twist that is uniquely yours.

The Missing Piece—The Story

If this was all there was to conflict, we would be in big trouble. But there's another element—the story. Your story is the way you understand the event. In this example, your story is that Chris purposely betrayed your trust in order to gain points with Morgan.

When someone does something that impacts us personally, we instantly interpret their behavior in a certain way. Our interpretation, which I am calling our story, is influenced by many factors including (but not limited to) our previous history with the other person, our mood on that day, childhood experiences, and our general level of trust in others.

Our feelings and our story are closely connected. But they are not the same, and it's important to distinguish between them. We could say that our feelings arise from our story. And although our feelings are valid, our story is based on limited information and there is a chance that it's incomplete or incorrect.

We have the power to find out. How often has your story changed when you learned something new? In the above example, suppose you learn that Morgan raised the subject with Chris because she already knew your information from another source. Would this piece of information not affect how you view the situation? And then would your feelings not change as a result? You still might not like people talking about you behind your back, but you no longer see Chris as the culprit. Also, you realize that your information is "out there" and no longer under your control (much to your dismay).

This is the choice point in a conflict. Are you willing to step into the unknown and consider the possibility that there's more going on than you know? If you are willing to do this, then you have something to work with because any new information you receive has the potential to alter your story and give you a larger perspective on the situation. As this happens, your feelings start to settle down. That can be the beginning of reconnecting with the other person and resolving the conflict.

Alternative to Reaction: Response

When your reaction is automatic (such as attack, avoid, or self-blame), it is a "knee-jerk" reaction as described in Chapter 3. When you go down that road, you have not inserted a pause and you have not made a conscious choice.

When you insert a pause and make a choice about what to do, you are *responding* rather than reacting. Being intentional about your response enables you to move *through* the conflict rather than unconsciously acting out your ingrained patterns. Moving through the conflict means actively engaging with the other person about the issue, being curious about their perspective while also being true to yourself. It does not mean discounting your emotions, nor does it involve blaming the other person. *This approach is the basis of Courageous Communication.*

A Four-Step Model of Conflict

To summarize, the four distinct components of conflict are:

1) Event
2) Story
3) Feeling
4) Reaction/Response

Something happens, we tell ourselves a story about it, a feeling arises within us, and we either react automatically or respond intentionally. All of this can happen very, very quickly. Of these four steps, the two steps you have the power to control in the moment are the story you believe about the event and your response—steps number 2 and 4. Indeed, you can use your *response* to check out your *story*. Any new information you receive has the potential to influence your *feeling*.

Crossing the Bridge

We can think of conflict using the analogy of a bridge. Suppose that you and the other person live on opposite sides of this bridge. You have a whole world of experience on your side of the bridge, a world that hangs together in a way that makes sense to you. You know the streets and the houses, the neighbors, trees, and pets. You know the weather patterns and the configuration of stars in the sky. You know the route to the grocery store, the medical clinic, the gas station, and all the other landmarks. All this is so familiar to you that you don't think about it or even notice it.

The other person is just as familiar with the world on their side of the bridge. They know the streets and the houses and all the rest. They know it as well as they know their face in the mirror. But their world is different from yours, perhaps so different that it seems like a different planet to you.

When you are in conflict with this other person, it is tempting to interpret their behavior from the perspective of your side of the bridge. When you respond rather than react, trying to learn more about their perspective, you are choosing to cross the bridge to their side and experience their world for a while. When everything inside you wants to be right, to get your way, or to be the "good guy," you are called to reach out and consider the possibility that there is another point of view that is just as valid as your own. At the same time, you open to the possibility that their actions are not purely malicious.

Crossing the bridge does not mean that you agree with them, nor does it mean that you are permanently abandoning your own point of view. You are trying to see the bigger picture. To do this, you do your best to suspend your story, your preferences, your certainty, and even your anger. You temporarily park these and try to be present *with the other person.* You are going against your ingrained habits, which is hard.

But you do it anyway. You go to that uncomfortable place and you stay there for a while. As best you can, you pay attention to what you see and hear on their side.

You cross the bridge not as an intruder, but as a guest. You are not asking them to justify their behavior, nor are you asking them to provide you with every detail. *You are asking them to help you understand their perspective.*

As a guest on their side of the bridge, you tread carefully. You listen in order to learn. If they need time to think, you allow the space for that to happen. Perhaps, out of respect, you retreat for a time, conveying your willingness to return when they are ready.

When you commit to working with conflict proactively, you take on a significant and meaningful task. Part of that task is making a sincere effort to see the other person as they see themselves. As best you can, you put aside your own perspective for a time. Trusting that "all behavior makes sense," you accept the challenge to discover "Why?"

A spiritual reference for this approach is beautifully expressed in the Prayer of St. Francis of Assisi, which includes the following passage:

> *O divine Master, grant that I may not so much seek*
> *To be consoled as to console,*
> *To be understood as to understand,*
> *To be loved as to love...* [xii]

This way of thinking is also expressed in Habit 5 of Stephen Covey's *The Seven Habits of Highly Effective People*, which instructs us to "Seek first to understand, then to be understood."[xiii]

When you embrace this philosophy by spending time on the other side of the bridge, sooner or later something begins to shift. Your sincere attention helps the other person to relax, easing the tension between you. At the same time, you learn new information that helps you to gain a better understanding of their perspective.

There are times when crossing the bridge may be inappropriate—for example, if there are issues of physical or emotional safety and you need to create a boundary. Most of the time, though, crossing the bridge helps you in at least two ways: it expands your thinking and it helps to ease the strain of a conflict situation. And each time you go across, it makes it easier to cross similar bridges in the future.

Crossing Back to Your Side of the Bridge

Once you sense that the other person has started to relax, you can invite them back across the bridge to your side and tell them how you see the situation—what it looks like in the context of your world.

How do you know when to bring them over to your side? Actually, you do not know for sure. You rely on your instinct and sometimes you just guess. If you try to explain your perspective and they resist you, then they are not yet ready to make the journey to your side of the bridge. No matter how clever you are, no matter how forceful or how convincing, nothing you say will get through to them because they are not ready to hear you. So you go back to their side of the bridge and continue to listen for a while longer.

Does this take patience? Yes. It also takes courage, humility, and perseverance. Even done imperfectly, though, in the long run it usually pays off to stay on the other side of the bridge for longer than you would like.

Then, finally, a shift can happen that feels like magic—once the other person feels truly heard, they sometimes become willing to hear your perspective. They might even invite you to speak.

Before I started practicing the skills of Courageous Communication, I had never experienced someone asking me about my perspective in the midst of a conflict. It seldom happened even in normal conversations. Now, it happens frequently. The first time someone spontaneously asked me what I thought, I was astonished. It strengthened my commitment to the approach I was practicing, and it reinforced my belief in people's basic goodness.

Sometimes, though, they just keep talking. If I spend all my time on the other side of the bridge, I grow resentful. This is not helpful to me or to anyone else. So while I make an effort to stay on the other side of the bridge for longer than is comfortable, I don't try (or pretend) to stay there forever. At some point I ask the other person if I could now explain my perspective. This usually gets their attention. Because I listened to them, they are now willing to listen to me.

If they express no willingness to hear my perspective, I end the conversation for the time being. Ending the conversation does not mean that I give up. It just means that I am taking a break. I remain open to the possibility of dialogue that is more balanced after a cooling-off period.

The Dance of Conflict

In the dance of conflict, you sense the other person's moves and adjust your own accordingly. There is give and take, forward and backward motion. As the process unfolds, you and your partner gradually find the rhythm that works for both of you.

At first, you might have to give more than you get. Such is life. You use Courageous Communication for the long game, as uncomfortable as that can be in the short run. You put aside your immediate agenda for the sake of your relationships and your own inner journey. Of course, there are times when you need to set a boundary or otherwise protect yourself. But for most conflicts, treating them as a dance leads to better outcomes than making a declaration.

This takes us to the heart of Courageous Communication. Courageous Communication is only rarely about getting your way, and it never has anything to do with convincing others of your position. On the other hand, it is also not about bowing to another's point of view. Courageous Communication takes us beyond the notion of winning and losing altogether.

In the beginning, conflict feels like "you against me." As you and the other person learn to dance together, at some point the conflict often shifts. You can feel something click into place, and at the same time there's a spontaneous sense of connection. Instead of "you against me," the conflict becomes "you and me against the problem." The sense of alienation shifts to one of understanding. Neither of you is victorious over the other; both of you share victory over the conflict itself. From this point on, the two of you are solving "the problem" together.

Part III

Preparing to Cross the Bridge

Chapter 8

Learning the Skills

*"I am always doing that which I cannot do, in order
that I may learn how to do it."*

—Vincent Van Gogh

From the beginning of my formal training in conflict resolution, I practiced the skills I was learning in my everyday life. With colleagues, clients, friends, and family members, I consciously tried to incorporate the skills by changing the way I listened and the way I expressed myself. I wanted to understand the skills, and I wanted to be able to use them well. I knew that practice was the only way.

There's a First Time for Everything

During the time of my training, I worked as a realtor. One day I showed a property to prospective buyers, Saul and Ella. After the showing, Saul, Ella, and I went back to my office to discuss the property they had seen. I had recently returned from my first course, and I was determined to put the skills to use. Ella said, "I really like this property, but I think they are asking too much for it." The time had come. Feeling self-conscious and awkward, I said back to her, "So, you like the property, but the price seems high." I fully expected her to laugh in my face. To my amazement, she did not skip a beat. She said, "Yes, that's right..." and the conversation continued.

In that moment, I learned a powerful lesson. These skills *work*. Ella was not disturbed by hearing me repeat back what she had said. If anything, she felt relieved and validated. Perhaps expecting an argument from me, she had instead received an acknowledgement. I had gone to her side of the bridge.

Practice, Practice, Practice

The next several chapters will present concepts and skills that have helped me to heal relationships, and work with conflict, in a very practical way.[5] They are the tools in my communication toolbox. The skills themselves are simple. Most of them you probably already know. You may use many of them without thinking when you are feeling relaxed.

As we know, however, conflict is stressful. When we are under stress, we do not think well—we often react automatically rather than respond intentionally.

So if you want the skills to be available to you when you really need them, you must consciously practice them in your everyday life. As you practice the skills in low-stress situations, you will build different patterns of communication that will increasingly be available to you in times of stress.

I cannot emphasize this enough. Communication can be compared with playing a musical instrument. You may appreciate beautiful music, but in order to play it yourself you have to practice—a lot. You may like the idea of Courageous Communication, but to do it well you must practice it every day.

Discomfort is Inevitable

If you are like me, you will feel uncomfortable when you begin using the skills. They will feel awkward, even wrong, because they run counter to our "normal" way of communicating. Also, we fear how other people will react to us.

---

[5] All the skills of Courageous Communication are summarized in Appendix 1.

Don't let your discomfort stop you! It can help to try out the skills first in situations where you feel emotionally safe, such as with a close friend or family member. You can even tell people in advance that you will be using the skills, if that helps you.

You may find, as I did, that most of the time other people don't notice your self-consciousness when you are using listening skills. They may not notice anything at all. But at some level they sense that you are paying attention to them, which feels good to them, and any awkwardness on your part escapes their attention.

With practice, we improve over time. My son, Ryan, has told me that when I first started using the skills it sounded somewhat contrived. Now, he says he can hear the skills embedded in my speech but they sound completely natural. As the saying goes, "Fake it till you make it."

Talking to Yourself is Not Crazy

After a difficult conversation, you may realize that you reacted defensively. It can be helpful to practice saying things differently later, when you are alone. You could revisit the scene in your mind, think about a more skillful response, and practice saying it out loud. Say it more than once. This verbal expression strengthens your neural connections, and the skillful response you practice will be more available to you the next time you encounter a similar situation. Literally, you are reprogramming your brain. Our habitual patterns are deeply ingrained. It takes effort and discipline to create alternatives.

Similarly, if you are anticipating a stressful conversation, think about what you want to say and practice saying it aloud beforehand. You might even write it down. Just one sentence committed to memory can be very helpful when you are in a real situation and your emotions are strong.

Any time you encounter a new skill that appeals to you, whether in this book or elsewhere, practice it! To remind yourself, write it down and tape it to your bathroom mirror or your computer screen. You could also recruit a friend or family member to help you learn the skill.

Conflict-resolution seminars generally include verbal exercises and role plays; you could create your own.[6]

Personal Agency

I've been told by some people that nothing they say or do in certain situations ever makes a difference. They believe that they have tried *everything*, so there is no point in trying to use the skills and failing again. It seems to them that they have no agency in the situation.

But they don't know for sure until they step outside their comfort zone and use the skills. This became abundantly clear when I taught the skills of Courageous Communication to prison inmates.

Interpersonal dynamics in prison can be challenging. The inmates in my first class were certain that they would not be able to make any headway with staff members no matter how many skills they used. They also believed that they had few options for getting along with each other. The first time I taught the skills, the overwhelming response from the inmates was, "Are you kidding? These skills will never work here."

I replied, "Maybe you're right. But how will you know if you don't try? Then you can come back and tell me how it went." Some of the inmates in the class accepted this challenge. To their surprise, the skills worked! They found that they could ease difficult situations, build their sense of agency, and have better lives by using the skills—even in prison.

Feeling powerless does not always mean that you *are* powerless. Sometimes you have to step into the unknown to find out.

---

[6] Written exercises for many of the skills are given in Appendices 2-5.

Chapter 9

Stating Your Intention

"Our intention creates our reality."

—Wayne Dyer

Before we start talking about how to cross the bridge, let's consider the fundamental premise of this whole approach—the intention. The foundational intention of Courageous Communication, which can be invoked in tense moments and on which most of the skills are based, is the following:

"I want to sort this out in a way that works for both of us."

This short statement expresses your desire to move forward with the other person in a spirit of collaboration, working together to resolve the current challenge. You are acknowledging and respecting the other person while including your own perspective and interests.

When there is tension between you and someone else, it's entirely possible that they have a negative idea about your motivation. Stating what you hope to achieve can correct their misperception and shift the conversation in a positive direction. So when you are being misunderstood, or when a conflict is intensifying despite your best efforts, or when you don't know what else to say, *state your positive intention.*

Memorize It and Use It!

In a conflict situation, the statement "I want to sort this out in a way that works for both of us" might feel ridiculous—something you really don't want to say. I encourage you to memorize it and rehearse it anyway. If you have committed the statement to memory, then there's a chance you will remember to say it, or force yourself to say it, even if you don't believe it right then. And once you say it, you might realize that it is, indeed, what you really hope to accomplish.

This statement, which expresses the desire for mutual benefit, runs counter to the win-lose mentality that is embedded in the Western psyche. We have been conditioned to believe that what one gains, the other loses. In the midst of a conflict, it is difficult for us to imagine (or even desire) an outcome in which both people get their needs met. Nevertheless, time after time conflicts do get resolved in surprising ways when they are approached in this spirit of collaboration.

A Win-Win Solution to a Real Problem

A Baltimore neighborhood was experiencing vandalism by a group of young people. A local organization was called in to help. The organization held a meeting with all the people involved—the youth and the adults whose property was being vandalized. At the beginning, the meeting was heated as the adults vented their frustration and the youth reacted defensively.

A turning point came when the youth were asked why they did not hang out in the local park instead of in the streets. The youth replied that there was nothing to do in the park. One of the men present at the meeting suggested that they could play football. The youth were interested, but they did not know how to play the game. The man offered to coach them. The young people accepted his offer, and so a local football team was born. The vandalism in the neighborhood lessened dramatically, and fear and hostility were replaced by a feeling of community.

Win-win solutions emerge from seemingly intractable situations all the time. But it only happens if someone steps into the unknown by crossing the bridge or by stating a positive intention, or both. Sometimes one sentence is all it takes to change everything.

Overcoming Habits

Memorizing the statement "I want to sort this out in a way that works for both of us," and using it, helps you to make the transition from your habitual patterns to a more considered approach in conflict situations. If you have a tendency to fight, it can remind you that the other person's interests are just as important as your own. If you have a tendency to submit, it can remind you of the reverse: your interests matter too. If you tense up and shut down when things aren't going well, it can remind you to stay centered and open.

Remembering the intention of mutual benefit takes you away from blame. It validates both you and the other person, helping to create an environment of respect and openness. For long-term harmony in relationships, the statement of intention is not only effective, it is "do-able." You do not have to be a saint to make it work. You just have to try.

Getting Specific

You can also tailor your statement of intention to a specific situation. If you sense emotions rising—yours or the other person's—you could pause and ask yourself, "What am I trying to accomplish here? What's my intention?"

Something happens when you ask yourself this question. It refocuses you, helping you to step back and see the bigger picture. Then, when you say your intention, it can put an entirely different spin on the conversation. Consider the following examples:

- "I want to know what's important to you."
- "I would like to do a good job."
- "I want to help."

However you express it, conveying your positive intention is one of the most powerful tools in your communication toolbox. It's like a breath of fresh air, cutting through tension and misunderstanding. It reveals your sincerity and invites an authentic response from the other person. When in doubt, state your intention.

Frame It in the Positive

It works better to say what you *want* than saying what you do *not* want. Saying, "It is *not* my intention to…" can sound defensive. Think in terms of one of the following:

- "I want to…"
- "I'm trying to…"
- "My intention is to…"

If you must state your intention in the negative, try following your negative statement with a positive one. For example, if a conversation with your spouse is going down a familiar, painful road, you could say, "This feels familiar and I don't want us to speak to each other this way anymore. I want us to figure out a way to do it differently."

When Others Resist Your Efforts to Change

If you commit to changing your patterns of communication, people who know you will likely notice. Even if they have complained about your poor communication in the past, your use of the skills might feel uncomfortable to them. So despite your sincere efforts and good intentions, they may protest. They may question your ability to change, or they may attack or ridicule you. Psychologist Harriet Lerner refers to this as the "Change back!" reaction.[xiv] It is a defense mechanism that sometimes arises when people are confronted with change over which they have no control. They prefer their dissatisfaction with the old pattern over their discomfort with the new one.

If this occurs, you could respond with a statement of intention. For example, suppose you use a skill with someone near and dear to you who then says, "Don't pull that stuff on ME!" You could respond with one of the following:

- "I want to improve my communication skills so that we get along better."
- "I'm trying to communicate better."
- "I want to do my part to improve our relationship."

Putting your intention out on the table without aggression can disarm people. Doing it can feel risky, though, because you are exposing yourself. Try doing it anyway. In a strange way, it gives you confidence because you know what you want and are putting it out there. While there are no guarantees, often a surprising thing happens—other people appreciate your honesty and your commitment.

Raoul

Raoul was a maintenance manager in a large factory. A big, no-nonsense man, Raoul took great pride in his work. After a year at a new job, though, he was in danger of being fired because he was not getting along well with others—neither the people he supervised nor those to whom he reported. Raoul's employer sent him to me for coaching. After his first coaching session, Raoul cautiously told one of the maintenance-crew members that he was in training to be able to communicate with them better. To his surprise, the crew member replied, "Don't expect any kisses, but we'll try harder too."

Never Give Up

When you say, "I want to sort this out in a way that works for both of us," you are disclosing something about yourself. You might also hope that expressing your intention will have an effect on the other person, and that they will respond in kind.

Sometimes, perhaps often, this will happen. But it will save you much frustration if you realize that the other person might not respond in kind. Stating your intention is not a demand, nor even a request. It is self-disclosure, said to remind yourself as much as to inform the other person. Our intention does not change other people. Our intention changes us.

If stating your intention has no effect on the other person, do not give up. After a pause, try saying it again, or use another skill (see the following chapters), or step away and come back later. Sooner or later, something will shift, either in the situation or inside you.

You can do hard things.[xv]

Part IV

Skills for Crossing the Bridge

Chapter 10

Listening

"Deep listening is an act of surrender. We risk being changed by what we hear."

—Valarie Kaur

In Chapter 7 I talked about the importance of crossing the bridge. So how do you do that? The first skill for crossing the bridge is *listening*. Listening is an act of generosity, a gift to the other person. You put aside your own story for a time and commit to learning about another's point of view.

Most of the time, many of us do not listen well. While the other person is talking, we are often mentally formulating our response. In conflict situations, we may not listen at all. Our habitual reactions can take over and we might withdraw, fume silently, try to appease the other person, or talk right over top of them.

We can do better. We can reach across the gap that separates us from the other person and really try to understand what they are saying.

You might not be ready to listen to a particular person, or to anyone. There might be so much pain or trauma in your past that you are still tending to your own wounds. At a certain point, though, you might be ready to hear what others have to say. If and when you get to that point, it's possible that you will discover a freedom that you never dreamed possible—the freedom of moving beyond the constraints of your past. Listening can be part of your journey of healing.

Done well, listening is an art. You adjust your listening to suit the moment, and to suit your personal style. This chapter will explore four different ways to listen well. They are:

1) Silent listening
2) Prompting
3) Repeating back
4) Summarizing

These four skills are progressive in that each skill is more proactive than the one before. However, they are not progressive in terms of effectiveness—each skill is uniquely effective when used appropriately. And the first skill, silent listening, is sometimes the most effective one of all.

1) Silent Listening

When you listen silently, you give your full attention to the other person without saying anything. You cross the bridge and let your awareness be with them, in their world, as they see it. When you notice that your mind is wandering, bring your attention back to what they are saying.

As you do this, pay attention to your body language. Maintain an open, relaxed posture and make regular eye contact. This keeps you engaged and sends the message that you are giving them your full attention.

If you get bored or irritated or have an overwhelming urge to ask a question or give advice, just notice that thought and bring your attention back to what they are saying. You could even try saying nothing when they stop talking. Your silence can create a space in which the other person might feel comfortable enough to open up a bit more and reveal something that they have been holding back.

It is especially difficult to listen to others when you are under stress or in conflict and your mind is rushing around looking for ways to justify your position or defend yourself. But conflict situations are times when listening can be especially helpful. When you really understand where someone else is coming from, it can alter your perspective of the conflict—your story—and make the situation more workable.

The power of silent listening is well known by those who work with people in distress. Hospice workers and crisis counselors can spend much of their time listening, listening, while their clients give voice to their pain, confusion, and fear. When the client's emotions become too intense for words, listening can continue through extended moments of compassionate shared silence. For the client, being listened to in this way is an important part of their journey toward healing.

I once heard Pema Chödrön, a Buddhist nun, tell the story of a woman named Emily whose face and body were badly burned in a fire. Family members and friends came to Emily's hospital room with gifts and reassurances that her life would soon be back to normal. But they avoided looking into her eyes or listening to her. Despite her visitors' good intentions, Emily began to feel invisible. It seemed to her that no one had any idea what she was going through, and that no one really cared. After a time, she received a visit from a hospital volunteer who sat by her bed and listened while she spoke of her loss, her pain, and her fear for the future. Only when Emily was able to share in this way did she begin to feel a sense of acceptance and hope.[xvi]

2) Prompting

While silent listening can be appropriate and helpful, often we need to do more. One simple technique for encouraging the other person to continue talking is to "prompt" them. A prompt is a gentle request for more information, such as "Say more."

Prompting conveys an invitation from you demonstrating your sincere interest in their point of view. It gives the other person "the floor" for a while longer, creating a space in which they can delve further into their own thoughts.

I find prompting to be especially helpful when someone says something that doesn't make sense to me, or that seems flat-out wrong. Rather than immediately challenge them, I get curious. Remembering that all behavior makes sense to the person who is doing it, I invite them to tell me more about their perspective. If you have ever made an assumption that turned out to be wrong, causing havoc and misfortune, then this skill can give you a way to avoid that fate the next time you hear something that seems bizarre or incorrect.

The following are suggestions for verbal prompts. If you incorporate these sentences into your everyday speech, you might be surprised at what you learn about people you thought you knew well. Suggestions for prompts are:

- "Say more."
- "How so?"
- "Tell me more."

3) Repeating Back

With silent listening and prompting, you refrain from saying much at all. After a while, listening in this way might begin to feel one-sided or awkward. With the third listening skill, repeating back, you say more. Your words, though, are still in the service of listening. What you say expresses only what you are learning about the other person's side of the bridge.

Repeating back means what it says—you tell the other person what you heard them say. When you repeat back, you demonstrate your interest in their point of view. You're also verifying that you heard them accurately, because they will correct you if you get it wrong.

The most common form of repeating back is to paraphrase what the person said. Here is an example:

- *(You hear)* "I've been going 100 miles an hour all week without a break!"
- *(You say)* "You've been busy!"

When people first learn the skill of repeating back, they often end their statement with an upward inflection. This turns it into a question—you are requesting confirmation that you got it right. For example, saying "You've been busy," with a downward inflection at the end, is very different from saying "You've been busy?" In general, it is more affirming for the other person if you repeat back as a statement rather than as a question. If you misunderstood them, they will let you know.

So when you repeat back, *end your statement with a downward inflection.* If you find yourself struggling to do this, you are not alone. I encourage you to do it anyway, because it makes a big difference. It sends the message that you are truly on their side of the bridge.

Here are two more examples:

- *(You hear)* "I lived with my family in Texas for a while in my teens."
- *(You say)* "You lived in Texas when you were younger." *(downward inflection)*

- *(You hear)* "This day has been extraordinary!"
- *(You say)* "You've had a good day!" *(downward inflection)*

The other way to repeat back is to say someone's exact words (changing the voice from "you" to "me" and vice-versa). Exact words work well if you are repeating back instructions someone has given you, or if you are confused by what the person said. Repeating back someone's exact words reassures the other person, and yourself, that you heard them correctly. Again, end your statement with a downward inflection.

Here is an example of repeating back someone's exact words. (From now on, the downward inflection at the end will be assumed.)

- *(You hear)* "I need you to do Job A first. If you have time, please start on Job B."
- *(You say)* "You need me to do Job A first and, if I have time, start on Job B."

You might be inclined to begin your repeating back with "I hear you saying that…" While there might be times when this is appropriate, in general I discourage you from starting your sentence with "I hear…." Saying "I hear…" is about you and your perception, and less about them and what they said. Repeating back without this opener is smoother and makes it truly about the other person. Indeed, it's so smooth that you might feel kind of invisible as they just keep talking. That's the point— you're on their side of the bridge, after all.

Adding an Opening Buffer

Repeating back is not the same as agreeing. If you don't agree with what the other person is saying, but you want to let them know that you are trying to understand them anyway, it can be helpful to begin your repeating back with a short opening phrase. You are making it clear that you are repeating back *their* words, not your own. Examples of opening phrases are:

- "It sounds like you…"
- "It seems to you that…"
- "So, from your perspective…"

Be careful with using opening phrases such as these. Often, they diminish the positive effect of repeating back. For example, saying "It sounds like you want more support from me" is less impactful than saying, "You want more support from me."

Here is an example of repeating back with an opening phrase. Suppose someone says to you, "You're making too many demands on me, and I can't handle the stress." Possible responses are:

- *(Paraphrase response)* "It sounds like you're feeling a lot of pressure from me right now."
- *(Exact words response)* "So, from your point of view, I'm making too many demands on you and you can't handle the stress."

With either response, your tone of voice and your body language should indicate sincere interest. If you are misunderstood by the other person, state your intention (as discussed in Chapter 9). For example, if they accuse you of being patronizing, you could say one of the following:

- "I'm trying to do a better job of listening."
- *(Or)* "I want to make sure I'm understanding you correctly."

Personally, I can't remember a time when I've had to do this—and I repeat back many times a day. But it's good to be prepared just in case.

Benefits of Repeating Back

Overall, repeating back has tremendous power to validate the speaker. It is like taking their words, wrapping them in a box, and giving them back to them as a gift. Acknowledging them in this way helps them to relax and move forward. If what you say is inaccurate in any way, you can trust that they will let you know. Then you can repeat back again.

Repeating back is especially helpful when you hear someone repeating the same point over and over. When we repeat ourselves, it's usually because we believe that we're not being heard. For example, suppose your friend keeps coming back to the statement, "I just don't understand her." When you realize that you have heard this sentence more than once, you could repeat it back to them: "You don't understand her." You may find that when you validate them in this way, they begin to relax. They sense that you "get" them.

Repeating back also serves as a buffer for your own internal reaction by giving you time to process new information. If you are reeling with the impact of a statement that has caught you off guard, taking the time to repeat back the statement gives you a chance to recover and respond appropriately rather than having a "knee-jerk" reaction. In this case, repeat back *slowly*.

Repeating Back is Hard

For many people, repeating back is the most challenging listening skill because it is so different from our normal way of communicating.

But its importance cannot be overstated. If you can overcome your resistance and train yourself to repeat back, you will be astonished at how this one skill will enrich, and even heal, your connections with others.

When people hear you repeat back their words, they interpret it as an indication that you are interested in what they are saying. Whatever discomfort you are feeling is not on their radar. When you repeat back, they typically don't skip a beat. They just continue talking because they know they have your attention.

4) Summarizing

Summarizing is a variation of repeating back. Summarizing is just what it sounds like: you say the key points from the other person's statement. Getting it right is less important than making the effort. They will let you know whether or not your summary is accurate and complete.

Some people tend to be long-winded—they may have numerous complaints, or they may just have a lot to say in general. When you summarize their words, you validate them in a surprising way. Here is an example:

- *(You hear)* "This job is really getting to me. My supervisor is never around, you know, and sometimes I need direction. I think he takes too much time off. And I miss working outside. This desk job just isn't active enough for me. You know how I used to walk and walk when I had my doggy day care? Well, I miss that. Oh yeah, and the pay is terrible. I don't know how single people live on these wages."
- *(You say)* "There are several things about this job that are difficult for you."

After summarizing, you can gracefully transition into expressing your own point of view, moving on to another subject, or ending the conversation. Consider the following possible responses to the longer statement above:

- *(You say)* "There are several things about this job that are difficult for you. My experience is quite different—this job is a good fit for me."
- *(Or you say)* "There are several things about this job that are difficult for you. Would you mind if I change the subject? There's something I need to ask you."
- *(Or you say)* "There are several things about this job that are difficult for you. Sorry, I need to go now."

Because you have let the speaker know that you were really listening, they likely won't mind you disagreeing with them, changing the subject, or moving on. Even if they feel cut off, you have given them some degree of validation to make it easier for them.

Summary

In conclusion, the first four listening skills are:

1) Silent listening
2) Prompting
3) Repeating back
    a) Paraphrasing
    b) Exact words
4) Summarizing

Chapter 12 will present two more listening skills. But first we'll take a short detour to discuss using language to get beneath the surface of things.

Chapter 11

Language of Experience

*"Out beyond ideas of wrongdoing and rightdoing
there is a field. I'll meet you there."*

—Jalaluddin Rumi

Courageous Communication gives us tools for enhancing and healing our relationships with others. As we know, relationships don't just happen on the surface. Indeed, the deeper we go, the stronger the potential for meaningful connection. So one way to strengthen our relationships is to reveal a little more about ourselves, and to be a little more curious about others.

We can do this using Language of Experience. With Language of Experience, we express, and listen for, how life is *experienced* by ourselves and others. We get out of our heads, where we are thinking about things, and into our bodies, where we are *experiencing* them. It's a slight shift, but a significant one. Making this shift can lead to increased insight, understanding, and connection.

Before we go further with Language of Experience, let's discuss another way of communicating: Language of Description.

Language of Description

When my son Ryan was a young child learning how to talk, he would point to things as a way of asking me to name them. One winter day we went out for a walk. He pointed to a bush in someone's yard, its green foliage contrasting with the snow all around. I said, "That's a bush." Ryan laughed, so I said again, "Bush." He chuckled infectiously, finding great delight in calling that thing a bush.

In this way, Ryan was a typical toddler. The first words we learn are nouns: mama, daddy, table, chair. The next words we learn are verbs describing the actions we see; after that we learn adjectives. Ryan's first sentence, uttered many months later, was "Amber picked pretty flowers."

For the first part of our lives, then, we primarily use concrete, descriptive language. In standard English, and in many other languages, "thingness" continues to be emphasized as we go through life. For example, we say "Dinner was good," or "That book is boring," or "Casper is lazy/aggressive/foolish." This way of speaking, which I call Language of Description, describes the *qualities* of things as we perceive them.

Language of Description can get tricky, though, if the other person has a different view of the situation. For example, suppose I say, "It's a beautiful day," and Heather responds by saying, "It is not a beautiful day! It won't be beautiful until we get some rain!" Heather and I are expressing two incompatible points of view, and we cannot both be right. Either it is a beautiful day, or it is not.

Having a difference of opinion does not always create problems. But when we feel strongly about something, we can take offense if someone disagrees with us. Our sense of comfort evaporates, tensions build, and before we know it we are in conflict. Strong feelings can arise even when we are talking about something relatively unimportant. Suppose Sally says, "That was a great movie" and Harry replies, "No it wasn't! It was a TERRIBLE movie!" Then Sally and Harry could be on their way to a fight. Neither Sally nor Harry thinks that the movie is a big deal, but they fight about it anyway.

Speaking About Your Experience

With Language of Experience, we don't describe the way we *perceive* something. Instead, we describe the way we *experience* it. We speak about our inner process, our feelings, or our preferences.

For example, instead of saying, "That was a great movie," Sally could say, "I enjoyed that movie." By speaking in this way, Sally is shifting from a statement about the movie to a statement about herself, and there is no basis for disagreement. Harry is not likely to tell Sally that she did not really enjoy the movie. And if he does say this, then Sally can re-affirm her experience without making a statement about the movie or about Harry.

Language of Experience emphasizes the relational quality of things: "I savored every bite of dinner," "I became bored with that book," "I feel frustrated about what Casper is up to right now." When we speak in this way, we limit our comments to the only thing we can talk about with genuine authority—ourselves. And even though we're talking about ourselves, Language of Experience strengthens our connections with others because we're sharing something closer to our personal truth.

If others' experience is different from ours, Language of Experience provides us with a way to talk about our differences without animosity. Other people are less likely to take offense when we talk about our personal experience than when we proclaim our point of view as though it were a universal truth.

Language of Experience invites us to cultivate a deeper awareness of ourselves and eliminates all elements of blaming, judging, and analyzing others. It strips away our self-righteousness because there is no right or wrong in felt experience. Language of Experience helps us to relate honestly with things as they are in that moment.

Listening for Someone Else's Experience

We can use Language of Experience not only to express ourselves, but also to understand others. If my friend Karl says to me, "My boss is a tyrant!" I could respond with, "It sounds like you're having a hard time with him." In this way, I shift the conversation away from blaming Karl's boss, and I connect with Karl in a way that could help him to feel seen in his distress.

Without this approach, Karl might be inclined to go on with a litany of complaints about his boss. His complaints keep him feeling angry and powerless—a victim. Acknowledging his experience shifts the focus away from complaining. It helps Karl to look inward, which might help him to gain insight and to find his way through a difficult situation.

It also keeps me on track. What if Karl's boss is a friend of mine? Using Language of Experience does not prevent me from tightening up as Karl is speaking. Through my tightness, though, perhaps I could still be curious. When I acknowledge his experience, I support him without agreeing with him and without trying to fix the situation or getting lost in my own perspective.

A Way to Move Forward

I don't use Language of Experience all the time. But I use it often, and using it has helped me to open, learn, and grow. When I shift away from opinions (or even "facts"), and think in terms of experience, I'm more self-aware. In turn, I'm less likely to pass judgements on myself or others and more willing to cross the bridge.

Specific skills for using Language of Experience will be presented in Chapters 12, 15, and 18. This approach also informs many of the other chapters going forward from here.

Language of Experience alleviates some of the limitations and conditioning that are buried within me. I have more freedom; I have a choice. With Language of Experience, I can choose to step outside my conditioning and look at the world, and myself, with fresh eyes.

For me, it's really no choice at all.

Chapter 12

Listening More Deeply

"Every being needs to be listened to, loved and understood."

—Tara Brach

The final two listening skills are rooted in Language of Experience. Using these skills helps the other person to relax and open up, and strengthens your connection with them. Continuing with the skills numbering from Chapter 10, these final two skills are:

> 5) Reflecting back experience
>
> 6) Reflecting back the unmet desire

5) Reflecting Back Experience

Chapter 10 included instructions on different ways to repeat back what someone says to you. The skill of "repeating back" is about the *content* of what they say. With the skill of reflecting back experience, you listen for the *experience* that lies beneath their words.

As with repeating back, use a downward inflection at the end of your statement to indicate acknowledgement rather than a question. Here are some examples:

- *(You hear)* "This situation is unbearable."
- *(You say)* "You don't like it at all."

- *(You hear)* "I'm so glad that's over."
- *(You say)* "You feel relieved."

- *(You hear)* "I might as well be talking to a wall!"
- *(You say)* "You're frustrated."

This level of acknowledgment nourishes people. Connecting with someone at the level of their experience lands you squarely on their side of the bridge, and they know it. A famous reminder is that "people will forget what you said, people will forget what you did, but people will never forget how you made them feel."[xvii]

Following is a list of some possible words for reflecting back experience:

- Mad—irritated, frustrated, angry, enraged
- Sad—hurt, disappointed, unhappy, miserable
- Glad—pleased, happy, relieved, proud
- Anxious—stressed, tense, worried, overwhelmed
- Afraid—scared, frightened, terrified, panicked
- Ashamed—embarrassed, foolish, self-conscious, humiliated
- Surprised—shocked, stunned, taken aback, gob smacked
- Uncomfortable, upset, & concerned—*good catch-all words for difficult emotions*

As this list shows, reflecting back someone's experience often involves using emotional language. But Language of Experience is flexible—you can adjust your response to suit the person and the situation. There are many ways to reflect back someone's experience without naming feelings. For example, consider the following:

- "That hit you hard."
- "You're on top of the world!"
- "You're having a difficult time right now."

Notice the possibility of adding "right now" to the end of your statement, as in the last example above. If someone is having a hard time, adding "right now" to your reflective response is a subtle reminder that this, too, shall pass.

Another way to reflect back experience is to use verbs indicating attraction (e.g. like, love, enjoy, appreciate) or verbs indicating aversion (e.g. don't like, resist, push back). For example:

- "You love having your family home for the holidays."
- "You don't like being put on the spot."

Whether you use adjectives, verbs, or some other form of expression, reflecting back someone's experience opens the door to greater understanding, deeper connections, and more open conversations.

With this skill, you can sometimes begin with an introductory word or phrase such as "So..." or "It sounds like...." Then you name the feeling or experience that you are sensing. Following are some statements said to you, followed by possible reflective responses:

- *(You hear)* "I'm never going to get this right."
- *(You say)* "It sounds like you're feeling discouraged."

- *(You hear)* "I've been waiting around all day for you, and now you're not even coming!"
- *(You say)* "So, you're pretty frustrated right now."

- *(You hear)* "That was a great movie!"
- *(You say)* "Sounds like you really enjoyed it."

As with repeating back content, accuracy in reflecting back someone's experience is not required. When you name what you think someone is experiencing, and the word you choose doesn't quite work for them, they will correct you and say a word that works better. Having the exact word is less important than the interest and care you show by trying.

Suppose, for example, Terrice tells you that she has just been to a meeting that was a total waste of time. You could say, "You were disappointed." She might say in return, "I wasn't disappointed, I was *frustrated*." Even though you have not named Terrice's exact feeling, you *have* succeeded in getting her to talk in terms of her experience rather than in terms of blame or judgment. Grounding the conversation in experience empowers Terrice at no one's expense, and it prevents you from having to take sides.

Notice that saying, "You feel like..." or "You feel that..." is *not* Language of Experience. Inserting the word *that* or *like* after "You feel" changes the sentence to Language of Description. For example, if you say, "You feel like this is a terrible situation," you are acknowledging their opinion but not their felt experience. A sentence that would be more consistent with Language of Experience would be, "You feel frustrated about the situation." So, if you begin a sentence with "You feel," follow it with a word or phrase that conveys felt experience.

A schoolteacher was working at his desk after school one day when the father of one of his students walked into the classroom. The father, visibly upset, began berating the schoolteacher for treating his daughter unfairly. The schoolteacher remained seated and just listened, looking up at the man who towered threateningly over his desk. Eventually the teacher said, "You really love her, don't you?" Hearing that, the father started to cry.[xviii]

Reflecting back experience is more than a script; it is connecting with others in a way that is meaningful to them. That said, there might be times when people resist your attempt to shift the conversation away from their complaint and towards their felt experience. They are looking for agreement rather than emotional acknowledgement. When that happens to me, a deeper conversation seems out of reach and I let it rest, perhaps changing the subject.

6) Reflecting Back the Unmet Desire

The final listening skill is to acknowledge another person's unmet desire—something they want. Such responses begin with "You want" or "You would like." For example:

- *(You hear)* "Since Juan started working a second job, he's never home."
- *(You say)* "You want him to be around more."

- *(You hear)* "Maria is always late."
- *(You say)* "You would like her to be on time."

- *(You hear)* "Why can't I have that?"
- *(You say)* "You really want it."

Someone's unmet desire is at the heart of their complaint, their tirade, or their sorrow. When you can discern this, and say it to them, it can be an effective way to help them relax and move on. At the very least, it can help them to feel seen.

When my children were small, they would sometimes ask for things they couldn't have. I trained myself to reply with, "You really want _____ (that cookie, that toy, to go somewhere…). You can't have it right now." If I was willing to give them what they wanted at a later time, I would also say that. They seldom protested. Acknowledging that they wanted something seemed to help them accept the fact that they couldn't have it.

Alice

Alice was having a hard time with the skill of reflecting back experience. She understood it conceptually and was surprised at how hard it was for her to actually do it. Still, she kept it in her awareness, building courage and waiting for an opportunity. Then, while at her job, Alice took a call from a dissatisfied customer. The man yelled at her for a long time as she just listened. He finally said, "I don't know why I'm acting this way." Alice dug deep and said, "You're frustrated." The customer said, "Thank you for treating me like a human" and went on to express deep gratitude to her.

Thrilled with her accomplishment, Alice reported back, "It worked!"[7]

---

[7] Exercises for reflecting back experience and reflecting back the unmet desire are in Appendices 2 & 3.

Chapter 13

Concluding Thoughts on Listening

"Perseverance, secret of all triumphs."

—Victor Hugo

The six listening skills of Courageous Communication give you six different ways to cross the bridge. As you practice the skills individually, you will develop a sense of when to use each one. To help you get started, though, following are some suggestions for when each skill might be most useful. Please refer to Chapters 10 and 12 for descriptions of the skills themselves.

1) Silent listening—This skill can offer powerful support when you are with someone who is experiencing intense emotions, especially grief.

2) Prompting (e.g. "Say more")—Use this skill when someone says something that seems strange, confusing, or out of place. Train yourself to ask for more information instead of jumping to conclusions.

3) Repeating back—This is the central skill of Courageous Communication, mostly because repeating back forces you to cross the bridge. You can use it in most casual and business conversations, as long as there is no strong emotional charge. This skill is particularly helpful if someone keeps repeating themselves.

4) Summarizing—Use this skill if someone has a lot to say.

5) Reflecting back experience—If you sense that there is some emotional charge to what the other person is saying, name what you think they might be experiencing in that moment. The stronger the charge, the more important it is to name it.

6) Reflecting back the unmet desire—Use this skill when someone is complaining. You can also use it if they are expressing frustration or disappointment, and you have some sense of what they truly want.

Listening Responses to Be Careful With (or Avoid Altogether)

There are seven common listening-type responses which you should be careful with, or even avoid:

1) Interrupting
2) Saying, "I'm sorry you feel that way."
3) Giving advice
4) Saying, "I understand"
5) Describing a similar experience of your own
6) Agreeing
7) Using the word "but"

1) Don't Interrupt

Everyone knows what it feels like to be interrupted—we don't like it. Try your best not to do this.

2) Don't Say, "I'm Sorry You Feel That Way."

Saying "I'm sorry you feel that way" conveys lack of respect, responsibility, or care. You can only apologize for yourself, not for someone else's feelings. If someone is upset with you, see the suggested responses in Chapter 20.

3) Be Careful About Giving Advice

After you have listened well, you might be tempted to share some of your own wisdom. Be careful about this! For example, suppose that your friend says to you, "Now that Sam is off to college, I don't know what to do with myself." You might be tempted to say, "Have you thought of taking up a hobby?"

Advice such as this often misses the point. Many years ago, a full-page *Peanuts* comic strip caught my eye. In the first panel, Charlie Brown says to Lucy, "I'm bored." The next several panels show Lucy giving Charlie Brown various suggestions: "Why don't you take Snoopy for a walk?" and so on. In the last panel, Charlie Brown says, "Lucy, don't you know that when people complain they don't want advice, they just want sympathy?" This bit of comic-strip wisdom is profoundly true.

But oh, how most of us love to give advice! My suggestion is to first repeat back what the other person has told you, or reflect back their experience. Doing this demonstrates your genuine interest in them, not just in their problem. Then *ask them if they would like to hear your thoughts.* If they say yes, go ahead. If they say no, or give a noncommittal response, then they are not ready to hear you.

4) Be Careful About Saying "I Understand."

When someone says to me, "I understand," I do not feel heard or validated. "I understand" is about them, not me. Rather than saying that you understand, *demonstrate* that you understand by using one or more of the six listening skills.

5) Be Careful About Describing a Similar Experience of Your Own

When someone is telling you about a painful experience, you might feel compelled to share your own, similar story. You might believe that doing this will help the other person feel less alone. In my experience, this seldom works as intended. Going to the other side of the bridge means trying to understand the other person's experience on their terms, not yours. If you share your own experience, again you are making it about you instead of about them.

Some time ago, I was grieving following the death of a family member. A friend listened and listened, giving me the sense that she was there for me and that she cared. The next time I saw her, she told me that she had lost a family member under similar circumstances. I was grateful that she had waited to tell me, supporting me selflessly through my own time of grief.

6) Be Careful About Agreeing

This is especially important if someone is complaining to you about another person. Even if you agree, expressing that agreement can pull you into taking sides in a conflict. When you tell someone that you agree with them, they will automatically assume that you are on their side. They might even tell others, which can make things difficult for you down the road. You can end up in a conflict that has nothing to do with you.

7) Be Careful About Using the Word "But"

Saying *but* sends a mixed message. For example, suppose someone says, "I see that this is difficult for you, but I can't do anything about it." We intuitively believe that the first part of the sentence—"I see that this is difficult for you"—is just the speaker's way to soften the blow of "I can't do anything about it." How differently we hear it if the speaker simply says, "I see that this is difficult for you." Nothing else is required.

If it's important to combine two opposing thoughts, try saying them in two separate sentences. "I see that this is difficult for you. Unfortunately, I'm not in a position to do anything about it." Another option is to replace the word *but* with the word *and*: "I see that this is difficult for you, and right now I'm not able to make it easier." By removing the word *but* you give equal weight to the two thoughts. You acknowledge the other person while conveying your own, alternate, perspective.

If it's appropriate, you can also add a positive note at the end: "I see that this is difficult for you, and right now I'm not able to make it easier. I wish I could."

Catching Someone in a Lie

What if you believe that someone has lied to you? If you value the relationship, this is a difficult situation that benefits from careful handling. You might be wrong. If you are right in your assessment, then you can reveal the deception in a way that makes it easier for the other person to acknowledge it.

First, repeat back what you heard them say that seemed untrue to you. Ask them if your understanding is correct. Many times you will discover that you heard them incorrectly, which will eliminate the need to go any further.

If they confirm that you did, indeed, hear them correctly, then state what you believe to be true about the subject. Say it simply and directly and include the source of your information. Follow your statement with something like, "I don't understand how both of these could be true," or "Help me to understand how both of these are true." Then be silent. If there is a good reason for the difference, they will tell you. If not, then you have revealed the deception without attacking them. Here's an example:

- *(You say)* "Henry, I thought I heard you say that the widget you bought online last month cost $100, the amount we agreed to spend. Is that right?"
- *(Henry's response)* "Yes, that's right."
- *(You say)* "Well, I just received our credit-card statement, and I'm seeing a charge for $165. I don't understand the difference."

This approach gives the other person the benefit of the doubt and minimizes your risk of personal embarrassment. On the other hand, if they have been deceptive then you have shifted responsibility where it belongs without rancor. In this case, see Chapter 16 for a discussion of how to express yourself in the conversation that follows.

David

David was aware that he often talked too much. He would find himself rambling in conversations, hoping that somewhere along the way he would say something helpful or interesting to the other person.

David had tried to limit his speech without success. I suggested that, rather than trying to say less, he shift his attention away from himself and pay more attention to others by doing a better job of listening. Then, when he spoke, he would have a clearer idea of what to say.

David started listening more and saying less. Over time, his communication became more authentic, playful, and to-the-point. And, in a familiar twist, as he became more interested in others, he started to feel better about himself.

Go Forth and Listen

Listening is an art. With practice, you will become better able to listen well and you will do it with more ease. The most important thing is to make an effort to see the other person as they see themselves, so that you really hear their words and the meaning behind them.

When clients and friends come to me for communication advice, they sometimes begin by saying, "I don't know what to say to get *through* to them. I have tried everything and nothing works. They're impossible!" Almost always, I encourage them to begin by listening better. They are consistently amazed at the difference this makes.

As the saying goes, "People don't care how much you know until they know how much you care."[xix]

Chapter 14

Asking Questions

*"The important thing is not to stop questioning.
Curiosity has its own reason for existing."*

—Albert Einstein

Curiosity enriches our lives by leading to new insights, opportunities, and discoveries. Asking questions is a way to give voice to your curiosity, and can enhance your connections with others. Asking questions is a different way to cross the bridge.

With the listening skills presented earlier, the other person discloses things that are relevant and interesting to them and you affirm their words or their underlying experience. Asking questions is different— you focus on the things that are relevant and interesting to *you*. You are still on their side of the bridge, but you are choosing which part of the landscape you want to explore.

Questions can be either *closed* or *open*. Let's begin with closed questions.

Closed Questions

Closed questions are questions with a limited range of possible answers (usually *yes* or *no*, but not always). They begin with words like *do/did*, *have/had*, or *is/was*. The following are examples of closed questions:

- "Did you do your homework?"
- "Have you been to Alaska?"
- "Is it blue or green?"

Closed questions serve you well when you want a specific piece of information. By limiting the range of possible answers, you remain in control of the conversation. You get the information you want from the other person, and no more.

Closed questions can be a subtle way to make social conversation or to solicit support for your position. "Isn't this a gloomy day?" "This situation is getting out of hand, don't you think?" By asking this kind of closed question, you are not really expressing interest in the other person's point of view. Rather, you are inviting them to agree with you.

Some closed questions have a bristly quality. For example, "Are you *ever* going to get this finished?" or "Did you insult me on purpose?" With questions such as these, the aggression is thinly veiled and there will likely be an equally aggressive response.

When you ask a closed question, you are usually not venturing very far from your side of the bridge. The answers you receive to closed questions seldom alter your perspective or expand your heart. And, clearly, some closed questions convey an adversarial tone and can promote conflict. If you feel your irritation building, or you sense that a situation is moving toward conflict, I encourage you to stay away from closed questions.

This brings us to the other type of question—open questions.

Open Questions

With open questions, you invite the other person to express themselves more fully. Open questions begin with *who, what, when, where, how,* or *why.* Here are open versions of the closed questions given above:

- "How is your homework coming along?"
- "Where have you traveled?"
- "What color is it?"

For the purpose of crossing the bridge, open questions generally work better than closed questions. For example, instead of asking, "Did you go to the movie?" you can ask, "Where did you go?" Instead of a "Yes" or "No" answer, the other person can tell you as much or as little as they like. They might say, "Well, I went out for dinner with Anton and then we went to the movie. Afterwards we went to a different restaurant for dessert and coffee."

When you ask an open question, you give up control of the answer. You ask the question and then you let go. You have no idea what the other person is going to say. Your open question indicates the general area of your interest, but their response could be anything at all. Open questions are more about what the other person wants to say than about what you want to hear.

Open questions can encourage creative thinking and wide-ranging responses. When people who are working together hit a roadblock, they can ask each other, "How do you think this problem could be solved?"

Shifting to Open Questions

When I first began conflict-resolution training, most of the skills were so foreign to me that I could not implement them, nor even remember them. But the technique of asking open questions seemed straightforward and was something that I believed I could train myself to do.

So I started asking open questions instead of closed ones. In fact, in order to train myself well, for a few weeks I asked *only* open questions. I got myself into some awkward situations—one time I asked my husband, "What groceries did you pick up today?" I really just wanted to know if he had bought milk.

But I persevered with open questions until they came more naturally to me. Many times, I would start to ask a closed question before I realized what I was doing. I would stop myself then ask an open question instead.

In this learning process I discovered two things. First, I discovered that open questions are not always best. For a simple exchange of information in a non-stressful situation, a closed question works just fine.

Second, I started to understand that other people saw the world differently than I did. I first mentioned this personal shift in Chapter 4, in the section entitled "All behavior makes sense." It was asking open questions that helped me to see that someone else's point of view was as valid to them as my point of view was to me. For when I asked open questions, people usually interpreted the question as an invitation to tell me what they thought. And they thought plenty.

When you ask an open question, then, the question itself is only the first part. The second part is to pay attention to the answer using the listening skills described in Chapters 10 and 12. When you do this, you invite the other person to reveal the depth and breadth of their experience. You "get out of the way" so that they can share their thoughts.

Sometimes, someone's response to an open question may surprise you and cause you to rethink the story you've been telling yourself. One of the first open questions I asked was, "What is going on for you right now?" I asked this question of my friend Sheila in an email. We had been in regular contact previously, but I had not heard from her in a while. I was concerned that she was pulling away from me.

Sheila's reply confirmed my fear. She was, indeed, pulling away from our friendship, and I was deeply hurt. This experience taught me another important lesson: open questions sometimes lead to answers that are difficult to hear. If you can let yourself hear these answers, despite your disappointment or frustration, then you are seeing the world as it is rather than as you would like it to be. For me, authenticity is more important than validation. I want to know what's really happening on the other side of the bridge.

Using Open Questions to Shift to Language of Experience

I feel uncomfortable when people disparage others in conversations with me. Suppose someone makes a statement like "Ebenezer is full of himself." Inviting a shift to Language of Experience, I might reply with "What's it like for you to be around him?"

Another way to shift the conversation using an open question would be to respond to their statement with, "What has he done to make you think that?" When they answer I can then say something like, "It upset you when he did that," acknowledging their experience of Ebenezer's behavior.

Asking open questions, then shifting to Language of Experience, helps you to understand the speaker better. If you are tempted to judge them for disparaging someone, this approach helps you to suspend your judgment and connect with them at a deeper level. Also, this approach relieves you of any pressure to agree with them.

In essence, you go to the other person's side of the bridge to find out what is in their heart.

Be Careful…

Open questions are not infallible. Just as a closed question can be asked aggressively, so can an open question. This is especially true of questions that begin with *why*.

In non-stressful conversations, there is no problem with asking "Why?" But in conflict situations, asking "Why" can be a cover for an attack. Saying, "Why did you do that?" can convey judgment and blame. Indeed, that could be the true meaning behind your question.

If you are in a conflict and you sincerely want to know the reason for the other person's behavior, then take ownership of the question by saying, "Help me to understand why you did that." Beginning with, "Help me to understand…" takes the sting out of the *why*. It softens the intensity of the question by making it about you instead of about them.

There is a second aspect of asking questions that can be problematic: asking too many of them. When you are fully engaged in a conversation, your curiosity may compel you to ask question after question. Even if your questions are open ones, the dialogue could start to feel like an interrogation—your interest in the information has superseded your interest in the speaker. For this reason, I suggest that you try to use questions sparingly.

A Suggestion for Responding to "I don't know"

When you ask an open question, or even a closed one, the other person may answer with "I don't know." When "I don't know" is the answer to your question, you might sometimes sense that a more revealing answer is near at hand. They may be reluctant to share it, or they may be struggling to find it themselves.

In this case, you can go a step further in eliciting an answer to your question. Suppose that your initial question to someone is, "You seem frustrated. What's going on?" If they respond with "Oh, I don't know," you could say, "If you did know, what would it be?" Often, gently nudging them in this way helps them to clarify their thoughts and feelings, or to share something that they have been holding back.

A Journey of Discovery

When I was in school, right through my college years, I sat in the front row in most of my classes and raised my hand frequently to ask questions. (Yes, I was THAT annoying student.) When I turned my curiosity towards other people and started asking open questions to learn more about them, my life opened up in a remarkable way. Asking open questions, and listening to the answers, has brought me insights and knowledge that were completely unknown to me before.

With curiosity and wonder, the adventure of life never runs dry.[8]

---

[8] Exercises for converting closed questions to open questions are in Appendix 4.

<u>Part V</u>

Skills for Your Side of the Bridge

Chapter 15

"I" Language

"Self-expression is the dominant necessity
of human nature."

—Dale Carnegie

While crossing the bridge is essential for effective communication, it's only half the story. You matter too. There will come a time to cross back to your side of the bridge, and this Part presents skills for doing that.

Although I am shifting gears, I want to make one final push for crossing the bridge. In most conversations, I cross the bridge *before* I express my own perspective or experience. By crossing the bridge first, I make sure that I clearly understand the other person's perspective, and I affirm them. This usually makes it easier for them to listen to what I have to say.

Whether you cross the bridge beforehand or not, there is a way to express yourself that is both authentic and effective. A simple guideline is to begin sentences with the word "I." For example, instead of saying, "You make me angry," you can say, "I feel angry."

Beginning sentences with the word "I" does not, by itself, get to the essence of the skill. The key for promoting authenticity and personal responsibility, especially in times of conflict, is to use "I" Language to reveal some aspect of your inner world. In other words, "I" Language is most effective when it is combined with Language of Experience. Talking about your personal experience keeps your self-expression grounded and real. It also limits any tendency you might have to blame others.

There are two ways to combine "I" Language with Language of Experience. You can either describe your internal, felt experience, or you can express your desire or preference. These correspond to listening skills 5 and 6 in Chapter 12 (reflecting back experience and reflecting back the unmet desire).

Following are detailed descriptions of these two uses of "I" Language.

1) Expressing Your Internal Experience

With this use of "I" Language, you answer the question, "How do I feel right now?" If your answer is something like, "I feel that he is out to get me," notice the allegation and re-focus on your internal, felt experience. Your self-awareness might then become, "I feel frustrated" or "I'm scared."

Here is another example. Instead of saying, "You're not making any sense," you could say, "I don't understand you" or "I'm confused." You shift the focus away from the other person and towards yourself, which conveys your message without disparaging them. You can use the same approach when you are speaking about others who are not present. "He ridiculed me" becomes "I felt embarrassed."

There might be times when you aren't aware of what you're feeling, or perhaps you recognize that you're feeling *something* but don't have words for it. In either case, you can gently bring your attention to sensations in your physical body. Pause, breathe, and focus inward. It might help to close your eyes. Gently attending to your physical sensations brings you back to the present moment.

Paying attention to your inner experience is especially difficult if you are in a stressful situation. In a tense moment, looking inward is likely the farthest thing from your mind. *That's why it is so important to pause.* Pause, breathe, and refocus. Doing this, and using "I" Language, can open the door to greater authenticity and connection. It can shift the tone of the conversation into one that's more workable for both of you.

Then what do you actually say? If you don't already have a vocabulary of "feeling" words, here are some suggestions:

- Mad—irritated, frustrated, angry, enraged
- Sad—hurt, disappointed, unhappy, miserable
- Glad—pleased, happy, relieved, proud
- Anxious—stressed, tense, worried, overwhelmed
- Afraid—scared, frightened, terrified, panicked
- Ashamed—embarrassed, foolish, self-conscious, humiliated
- Surprised—shocked, stunned, taken aback, gob smacked
- Uncomfortable, upset, & concerned—*good catch-all words for difficult emotions*

If this list looks familiar, that's good! It's the same list that was presented in Chapter 12 under "Reflecting back experience." The only difference is that now you're describing your own experience instead of someone else's.

Here are some examples of converting "You" statements to "I" statements:

- *("You" statement)* "You're being irresponsible."
- *(Alternate "I" statement)* "I feel frustrated about this."

- *("You" statement)* "You're stressing me out."
- *(Alternate "I" statement)* "I feel tense/worried."

- *("Other" statement)* "She let me down."
- *(Alternate "I" statement)* "I'm disappointed."

- *("Other" statement)* "He's a jerk."
- *(Alternate "I" statement)* "I feel irritated about what he did."

Notice that "I" Language sometimes includes references to others. When someone has provoked a reaction in you, it is fine (and often necessary) to refer to that person in order to communicate clearly. When you are speaking for yourself, though, your references to others stand in the shadow of the "I" or the "me." The other person's actions might be the catalyst, but your experience belongs to you.

There may be times when it does not seem safe or appropriate to use feeling words. At these times, you can express your inner experience another way. Consider, for example, the following responses:

- "My head is spinning."
- "It's hard for me to hear what you are saying."
- "I'm not in very good shape right now."

When you have no words for what you are experiencing, you could say, "Something is going on for me right now and I don't know what it is," or simply, "I feel uncomfortable." In a tense situation, *any* sincere statement of self-disclosure works better than a statement of blame.

Often, authentic self-disclosure also works better than saying nothing. When others can sense your tension and you say nothing, the silence can become a barrier between you. By giving voice to your inner process, you drop your guard and become more accessible.

"Right Now…"

If you want to acknowledge the transient nature of emotions, you could link your "I" statement with the present moment. That way you are not locked into anything in your own mind or in the perception of others.

- *("You" statement)* "You're full of it."
- *(Alternate "I" statement)* "Right now, I feel frustrated."
- *("Other" statement)* "He's obnoxious."
- *(Alternate "I" statement)* "I'm ticked off right now."

Noticing and expressing your inner landscape is a journey of self-discovery. As you lean into this practice, remember that *all feelings are valid*. Be gentle with yourself. We all feel things we would rather not feel, but ignoring or suppressing those feelings leads to blame and unresolved conflict. Your feelings are okay just as they are, they are no one's fault, and you're more normal than you think.

Ann

A young woman named Ann, a recovering alcoholic, was in a recovery program at a residential treatment facility. There were clear behavioral guidelines at this facility, including a prohibition against swearing.

Ann was participating in a weekly class on conflict resolution. She described herself as an angry person and was doing her best to apply what she was learning as a way to manage her anger. One day, Ann was sitting in a lounge at the facility with some friends. It was a relaxed, social time, with people coming and going. Caught up in a conversation, Ann used a swear word.

A few minutes later, a staff member named Carolle came into the room with an authoritative air. Looking at Ann, she said, "Someone in here swore and I bet it was YOU." Ann looked straight back at Carolle and said, "That hurt." Carolle replied, "Well, it was you, wasn't it?" Ann said, "Yes, it was me, but it still hurt."

When Ann told the story at our next class, she said that someone must have reported Ann's swearing to Carolle, who then entered the room in order to enforce a house rule. I congratulated Ann on staying present with what she was feeling, and expressing it, rather than attacking back. This was a significant, courageous step for Ann, and her directness had a surprising result. The day after the incident, Carolle approached Ann and said, "I haven't been able to stop thinking about what happened yesterday. I'm really sorry that I hurt you."

By speaking for herself when she was being verbally attacked, Ann had allowed a non-threatening space in which Carolle could reflect on her words and then apologize for them. Ann's response empowered both of them and transformed the dynamic between them.

Moments like this can change a relationship, or even change a life.

2) Expressing Your Desire or Preference

As discussed in Chapter 4, we all have preferences. We also have desires—there are things, and outcomes, we just want. Giving voice to your preferences and your desires is another use of "I" Language. Stating your intention, such as "I want to sort this out in a way that works for both of us," is one example of expressing your desire or preference (see Chapter 9).

You might think that what you want is obvious so why should you have to say it? And yet, what is obvious to you may not be obvious to others. Rather than retreating into frustration or self-righteousness, you could disclose what you're needing or wanting.

Statements in which you express your desire or preference usually begin with one of the following:

- "I want…"

  — *For example,* "I want to be with you."

- "I would like…"

  — *For example,* "I would like to get a puppy."

- "I would prefer…"

  — *For example,* "I would prefer to stay home tonight."

- "I would rather…"

  — *For example,* "I would rather buy a boat than take a vacation."

Sometimes it's helpful to include a time frame when you say what you want, such as "right now" or "when such-and-so occurs." Here's an example of converting a "You" statement to an "I" statement with a time frame:

- *("You" statement)* "This doesn't concern you."
- *(Alternate "I" statement)* "I would prefer not to discuss this with you right now."

Also, you can follow your self-expression with a request for action:

- *("You" statement)* "You never listen to me!"
- *(Alternate "I" statement)* "Right now, I'd like you to listen to me. Would you please do that?"

Finally, when you state your preference or make a suggestion, you can follow it with an open question inviting input from the other person:

- *("You" statement)* "You never ask for my opinion."
- *(Alternate "I" statement)* "I would like to be included in the conversation when decisions are being made. How would that work for you?"

With all these variations, the central instruction is to put yourself out there by *saying what you want or prefer*. Over time, you'll figure out the rest.

That said, there are times when it's better for you *not* to express your desire or preference. If others' needs are greater than yours at that moment, or if you don't feel emotionally (or physically) safe, you might choose not to say anything right then. In long-term relationships, though, your unmet desires can turn into frustration and disappointment if they are not addressed. It's usually better to voice them sooner or later than to stay silent and hope for the best.

This can feel uncomfortable, and doing it despite your discomfort can be an act of courage. You express your desire not as a demand, but as a request and a way to be authentic. Not knowing how the other person will respond is what makes it courageous.

Sometimes you might not know what you want. But if you are complaining, inwardly or outwardly, that means you want things to be different in some way. If you just can't figure out what you want, you could say, "I feel dissatisfied right now and I don't know what would make me feel better." Naming your dissatisfaction is a way to be kind to yourself, and it can be a relief to others—it lets them off the hook. If you don't know what you want, how could they? They might even offer you their support since there is no pressure on them to fix your problem.

For simple requests in low-stress situations, it can work well to frame your words as a question rather than as a statement. You can say, "Would you please…?" or "Would you mind…?" or "Would it be okay if I…?" By doing this, you give the other person more of an opportunity to say "No." If they comply with your request, or give you the go-ahead, they usually do so as a matter of choice. It's empowering for both of you.

My journey with "I" Language

Of all the communication skills I studied, "I" Language was the most challenging one for me to learn and use. The first time I was given an assignment to restate "You" statements as "I" statements, I simply could not do it. I was accustomed to hearing sentences beginning with the word "You," especially during times of conflict. Others expressed their anger towards me in statements like, "You did that on purpose!" I spoke, and thought, in similar language. Underlying my communication patterns was my belief that others were responsible for my feelings, and that I was responsible for theirs.

"I" Language challenged this deeply held belief and provoked a strong inner resistance. I justified my resistance with some Buddhist jargon, but my resistance was so massive it made me suspicious. What was my resistance really about? In an effort to answer that question, I decided to express myself using "I" Language for a while and see what happened. Maybe it would be useful.

"I" Language turned out to be way more than useful. For me, this skill was transformative. It exposed layers of internal conditioning and helped to loosen the grip of my preferences, my certainty, and my anger. Instead of fostering arrogance, as I feared, "I" Language helped me to gain a deeper understanding of humility.

Starting sentences with the word "I" required me to shift my focus away from the other person and pay attention to what *I* was experiencing. In conflict situations, this was especially hard. But when I made this shift, I would often discover an intense emotion that had been hiding from view. No wonder I resisted looking inside! But once I did, it was like coming home—I wasn't hiding behind blame and accusation anymore. To me, this is the essence of freedom.

Learning to Ask for What I Wanted

A pivotal moment in my life came when I was seeing a man named Ray. We dated for a while, then broke up. A few weeks later, we reconnected. After calling me a few times, Ray asked if we could get together on Friday night. I said yes.

But I had one problem. In the earlier phase of our relationship, Ray and I seldom went out. His idea of "getting together" was to come over to my apartment and spend the evening watching TV. So when Ray suggested that we get together, I knew what he meant—he wanted to come over to my place. I also knew that *I* wanted to go out. But I was afraid that if I asked for what I wanted, he would reject me. I decided to ask anyway. Having made the decision, I was terrified—the kind of terror that is about way more than the situation itself.

On Friday afternoon I received a call from Ray. Sure enough, he said, "Is it still okay if I come over tonight?" I had prepared for this moment by rehearsing my words over and over. Still, actually saying them was one of the hardest things I have ever done. I replied, "I would like to get together with you tonight, Ray, but I would like to go out." His reply floored me. He said, "That's fine with me. Where would you like to go?"

Making that one request changed my life. I discovered that I could, indeed, ask for what I wanted and the world would not come to an end. It was a moment of empowerment, one that I had created for myself. As my relationship with Ray unfolded, standing my ground became one of its hallmarks. Having done it once, I discovered that I could do it again and again without jeopardizing the relationship. I had found my voice.

Do It with Kindness

I used to try really hard to maintain an image of perfection, and when I fell short of that image I felt like a failure. "I" Language helped me to learn that I am more complex than that, and that being perfect was never the point. For when I keep trying to have it all together, I miss an important aspect of what it means to be human.

As I said earlier, a significant aspect of my personal practice is to love myself as I am. "I" Language helps me to let go of my concepts about myself and awaken to what is true for me in this moment, whether it is comfortable or not. When I do this with kindness towards myself, I'm better able to love and be loved.

Speaking this way can also create space for others, for revealing myself authentically can make them feel comfortable enough to do the same. When I drop my barriers, they can too.

There is more to each of us than we can ever know.[9]

---

[9] Exercises for converting "You" and "Other" statements to "I" statements are in Appendix 5.

Chapter 16

Expressing Dissatisfaction

"Criticism may not be agreeable, but it is necessary.
It fulfils the same function as pain in the human body.
It calls attention to an unhealthy state of things."

—Winston Churchill

In interpersonal relationships, dissatisfaction is inevitable. This chapter presents a way to express your dissatisfaction that is both honest and respectful. Using two or more steps of a four-step "DESC" Script, you state your concern while avoiding any form of blame or judgment. Often the first two steps are sufficient (the "DE" Script). Sometimes adding the third step is helpful (the "DES" Script). Occasionally, but rarely, all four steps are called for (the "DESC" Script).

Let's start with the first two. Then we will add the third, and finally the fourth.

Cause and Effect—the "DE" Script

The two elements of the "DE" Script are:

    1)   D—Describe the behavior you want to address
    2)   E—Effect of the behavior

First, you *describe* the other person's behavior in neutral language.

This part of the script begins with the word "When." For example:

- "When you called me incompetent..."
- "When you left your dishes in the sink..."
- "When you didn't respond to my message..."

Notice that you are not shying away from stating what happened, but neither are you making it into a bigger deal than it is. Your description works best if it is:

- *Specific*—a single event, or sequence of events, stated simply and directly just as it (or they) happened

- *Shared information*—if asked, the other person would agree that the event you're describing happened the way you said it did

- *Non-judgmental*—No emotionally charged language (just the facts)

The second part of the "DE" Script is the *effect* of the behavior. There are two ways to say this, depending on whom the behavior has affected:

- If the behavior has affected you personally, use "I" Language to describe that effect—your inner experience, your unmet desire, or both

- If the behavior has affected others, state the specific effect on them

Consider the following accusing statements and the "DE" Scripts that could be used instead:

- *(Accusing statement)* "You are out of line."
- *(Alternate "DE" statement)* "When you take my things without asking me *(describe behavior)*, I feel frustrated *(effect)*. I want to be able to trust you *(unmet desire)*."

- *(Accusing statement)* "You're ruining this project."
- *(Alternate "DE" statement)* "When you don't complete your part of the project on schedule *(describe behavior)*, the whole team scrambles to cover for you *(effect)*."

- *(Accusing statement)* "You're driving me crazy!"
- *(Alternate "DE" statement)* "You told me that you would be finished by 3:00 so we could go out. It's now 4:30, and you're still working *(describe behavior)*. I'd like to get going *(unmet desire)*!"

- *(Accusing statement)* "You're too withdrawn."
- *(Alternate "DE" statement)* "It's hard for me *(effect)* when you don't say anything *(describe behavior)*."

Note that the Effect ("It's hard for me") can come before the Description ("when you don't say anything").

This script can be especially useful as a replacement for a common misuse of "I" Language: saying "I feel that you..." or "I feel like you...." What follows is often an accusation of some kind—for example, "I feel like you're not pulling your weight." This kind of a sentence is not Language of Experience because no personal experience is stated—you're actually blaming the other person even though you began the sentence with "I feel."

Instead, use a "DE" Script: "When you extend your coffee break, I have to cover for you. I'm not able to get my own work done and I'm feeling frustrated."[10]

What is the difference between a "DE" Script and blaming? With a "DE" Script you are describing the person's behavior not to find fault, but to share its effect on you. You are not judging the person, nor are you second-guessing their motive. And you do not blame them for your

---

[10] Saying "I feel like/that..." can be an effective way to convey an intuitive observation, for example, "I feel like we're making progress." The suggestion here is to avoid saying "I feel like/that" followed by an accusing 'you' statement.

reaction; you claim your experience as your own. Your self-disclosure invites the other person to your side of the bridge, after which you may willingly go to theirs.

Adding a Third Step—the "DES" Script

Often, the "DE" Script is sufficient to get the other person's attention. Depending on your relationship with them and the circumstances, you can add a third step to drive the point home. The optional third step is to "Specify" the behavior you would prefer. The "DES" Script is therefore:

1) D—Describe the behavior you want to address
2) E—Effect of the behavior
3) S—Specify the preferred behavior

In the entire script you avoid blame or judgments and you stay away from the word "should." Here are some examples of statements that follow the "DES" Script:

- "When you tell me only the things I did wrong *(describe behavior)*, I feel discouraged *(effect)*. I want to do a good job, and I would appreciate some encouragement *(unmet desire)*. Would you please also tell me what I did well *(specify preferred behavior)*?"

- "When I hear you criticize my family *(describe behavior)*, I pull away from you *(effect)*. I would appreciate it if you would lighten up towards them *(specify preferred behavior)*."

- "I feel uncomfortable *(effect)* when you ask me to stretch the truth for you *(describe behavior)*. I would prefer to stay out of this altogether *(unmet desire)*. Would you please not ask me to do that again *(specify preferred behavior)*?"

The "DES" Script gives you a method to express your dissatisfaction, and to ask for what you want, in a way that is both truthful and non-blaming.

Adding a Fourth, Final Step—the "DESC" Script

There might be times when you need to be especially firm and clear, letting the other person know that you will no longer tolerate certain behavior. At such times, you can add a fourth step: "C" for the "Consequence" of non-compliance. The "DESC" Script is therefore:

1) D—Describe the behavior you want to address
2) E—Effect of the behavior
3) S—Specify the preferred behavior
4) C—Consequence of non-compliance

The "DESC" Script can be effective in situations of clear power differentials, when you are in charge and you need to make a clear statement to someone under your supervision. Here are two examples:

- *(Parent to teenage child)* "When you stay out past the time we agreed to *(describe behavior)*, I feel upset and worried *(effect)*. Please come home on time *(specify preferred behavior)*. If you stay out late again, I'm going to ground you for two weeks *(consequence of non-compliance)*."

- *(Supervisor to employee)* "When you don't clean up after yourself in the shop before you leave for the day *(describe behavior)*, someone else has to do it for you *(effect)*. I would like you to clean up at the end of every shift *(specify preferred behavior)*. If you leave a mess again, I'm going to let you go *(consequence of non-compliance)*."

In most relationships such as these, stating a consequence happens rarely—a more conciliatory approach generally suffices and is easier for everyone. If you decide to state a consequence, though, *you must be prepared to follow through*. If you state a consequence but don't follow through, you have weakened your position and the behavior is sure to continue. So stating a consequence should not be done lightly.

The other use of the "DESC" Script is in the rare, extreme situation with a close friend or intimate partner where you value the relationship but have reached your limit and are committed to change—one way or another. For example:

- *(To a close friend)* "When you canceled at the last minute for the second time *(describe behavior)*, it was too late for me to find someone else to travel with, and going by myself wasn't the same *(effect)*. I need you to give me more notice if there's any chance you might cancel *(specify preferred behavior)*. If you cancel on short notice again, I don't think we can plan anymore trips together *(consequence)*."

- *(To a spouse)* "When I find out you've lied to me *(describe behavior)*, I feel betrayed *(effect)*. This isn't the first time, and I want us to get help *(specify preferred behavior)*. If you won't see a therapist with me, I'm leaving *(consequence)*."

Stating a consequence in this type of situation is emotionally intense and can be scary. If you find yourself in an untenable situation, though, using this script allows you to express yourself with clarity and power. There's no mistaking the point you are making.

Again, don't say it unless you're sure you will follow through if things don't work out.

The Power of Giving Clean Feedback

When I taught communication skills as a prison chaplain, the two main takeaways for the inmates were the listening skills and the "DES" Script.

Incarcerated people must be very careful not to offend others in their world or bad things can happen. There can be fights with other inmates or disciplinary consequences if their attitude with staff is considered disrespectful. The inmates did not generally use the "Consequence" part of the script, but they did employ the first three steps to great effect. It gave them a way to give feedback and ask for what they wanted without jeopardizing their safety.

Even without stating a "Consequence," it can be daunting to contemplate using the "DE" or the "DES" Script. I encourage you to do it anyway, remembering to keep the "D" part neutral—just the facts as you both know them. In other words, don't get in a fight about the "D" part. The impact should always be in the "E" part, the Effect. With this approach you are sharing information rather than casting blame.

You can begin by thinking about a difficult situation in your life and compose a "DE" or "DES" Script to address it (or even a "DESC" Script). You don't have to actually say your script, just think about what you could say. Perhaps even write it down. Then do it for another difficult scenario. Eventually it will start to come more naturally, and you can use it in real life.

If it works inside prison, it can work for you.

Chapter 17

Saying "No" and Setting Boundaries

*"Boundaries aren't about telling other people what
they can or cannot do. They are about deciding what
you will or will not tolerate."*

—Unknown

Life is not always about getting along with others, and there are times when crossing the bridge, or even remaining neutral, is not appropriate. There might be times when you need to decline a request by saying "No," or attend to your wellbeing by setting a boundary.

When you say "No" or set a boundary with another person, you are asserting yourself in the relationship. You can send this message with an action, such as closing a door when you want privacy. Saying "No," or setting a verbal boundary, is as clear as closing a door. It is a firm statement, letting the other person know exactly what's OK with you, and what's not.

It's also possible to request or negotiate a boundary. These more nuanced approaches are covered in the section on "Expressing your desire or preference" in Chapter 15 and in the sections on the "DE" and the "DES" Scripts in Chapter 16. Of the skills presented so far, only the "DESC" Script in Chapter 16 is a way to set a non-negotiable boundary.

In this chapter, I present two other ways to assert yourself when you are clear about what you will or will not do, or what you will or will not tolerate from another person. First, I'm going to talk about saying "No" in response to a request. Second, I'm going to talk about setting a boundary in situations where you are experiencing, or anticipating, a violation of your personal space.

1) Saying "No" in Response to a Request

Have you ever said "Yes" to something when you wanted to say "No?" If so, you know how hard it can be to turn down a request from someone else. But being able to say "No" is essential for self-respect and self-direction. By saying "No" to others when you need to, you are saying "Yes" to yourself.

There are different ways to say "No," depending on the circumstances. Here are some options:

- "No."
- "I've decided not to."
- "Not going to happen."

Most of the time, you can offer an explanation with your "No." In tense situations, though, it's best *not* to explain yourself. Offering an explanation gives the other person an opening to challenge your reasoning. A famous quote reminds us that "The word 'No' is a complete sentence."[xx]

If you want to respond in a lighter tone, you can say one of the following:

- "Nope."
- "Probably not."
- "I'd rather not."
- "I'm not able to do that right now."

If it is hard for you to say "No," practice it! You can say it to yourself in the mirror, or practice saying it with someone you feel comfortable with. As you say your "No," try to maintain eye contact with them and keep an upright posture. Say it like you mean it.

You might be tempted to say, "I can't" or "I shouldn't." Such statements place responsibility for your decisions on something beyond your control. It is more empowering to take full responsibility for your choices by just saying "No" or one of its equivalents.

If the other person persists in their request, keep saying "No." Under pressure, speak more firmly and use their name. If you do not succeed in getting through to them, it is probably a good idea to end the conversation for the time being.

As with the other skills, building your capacity to use this skill takes time and effort. If saying "No" feels challenging to you, remember that *you can do hard things*.

DeAndre

DeAndre was engrossed in a project on his computer when his roommate, Henry, asked for some help with his taxes. For most of his life, DeAndre would have stopped what he was doing to help Henry. But he remembered that he was making an effort to be less accommodating of others when attending to his own priorities.

DeAndre told Henry, "Sorry, this is not a good time for me." Success!

Buying Time

One of my real-estate colleagues was a man named Armand. Armand operated at great speed and consistently conveyed a sense of urgency in his communication. When he wanted something, he wanted it right away and it was always VERY IMPORTANT. I am a slower person and was easily ruffled by Armand's demands. That is, until I learned to say, "I'll get back with you on that." If he continued to push me I would say, "If I give you an answer now, it will be no." That usually helped him to cool his heels.

2) Setting a Boundary in Response to a Personal Infringement

Setting a verbal boundary is for situations where someone is infringing on your well-being or your personal space. It does not matter whether or not the other person sees their behavior as an infringement. This is about your perception, not theirs. Consider, for example, the following:

- Someone is yelling at you
- Someone insists that you let them have their way despite your resistance
- Someone persists in offering you unwanted advice despite your polite efforts to dissuade them
- Someone's behavior is unacceptable to you in some other way, and you want it to stop

Situations such as these require a clear, direct response. Do your best not to meet their intensity with your own anger. Be prepared to be firm, though, and to hold the line. Otherwise, your unsuccessful attempt at setting a boundary will actually weaken your power.

Do not jeopardize your physical safety, or the safety of others. The wise use of boundaries includes recognizing when a situation is beyond your control and acting accordingly. Perhaps the best thing to do is leave. If that is not possible, temporary compliance might be the safest course of action.

Much of the time, though, we have more power to set a boundary than we think. One way to do this is to use the person's name and make a clear statement or request. For example, suppose someone is leaning on you hard with unwanted advice. You have done your best to listen and respond but the other person is on a roll, their enthusiasm growing. You could say, "Angie, please back off. I need to figure this one out for myself."

Many other situations with rising tension call for boundary-setting statements. Some possible examples of such statements are:

- "I need you to stop doing that."

- "I'm not going to talk about this with you anymore."
- "It sounds like you're blaming me and I want it to stop."
- "I can't handle this. I'm leaving." Then leave.

Responding firmly, yet non-aggressively, is another place where practice can help, since the need for boundaries can arise in situations where emotions are running high. If you believe that an upcoming conversation is likely to turn nasty, or if you repeatedly find yourself feeling verbally intruded upon by someone, take the time to plan an approach that includes setting a boundary. Imagine yourself in the situation and rehearse your boundary-setting line. Say it aloud with conviction. Write it down. Practice it over and over so that, in the real situation, you will be able to say what you mean.

Setting a verbal boundary is a gift to yourself and, in some ways, a gift to the other person. You feel empowered, and the other person receives a clear, non-blaming message. Not only do you *feel* empowered, you *are* empowered. You are being true to yourself in the most profound and simple way—you are protecting yourself from intrusion or harm.

Taken by Surprise

Sometimes you might be taken by surprise, with no time to prepare your response. Despite all my training and practice, I continued to freeze in the face of such unexpected verbal assaults. Fortunately, they do not happen often. But after I found myself, yet again, feeling helpless as someone verbally attacked me, I realized that I needed to be more proactive in preparing for similar situations in the future. So I started challenging myself several times throughout the day. I would pause and think, "What if someone were to verbally attack me right now?" I visualized standing up to this imagined adversary with confidence, meeting them eye-to-eye and protecting myself.

After several weeks of imagining myself responding assertively to someone's verbal aggression, I found myself in another difficult situation. In my role as a public agency hearing officer, a client did not like my decision and she reacted by launching into an enraged tirade at me. For a moment I froze. Then I realized, "Oh, this is what I've been preparing for." I straightened my posture and in a strong and steady voice I said, "You need to leave now." My words were unnecessary, for others were containing the situation, but they mattered to me. At last, I had overcome my "freeze" reaction to stand up for myself.

A Life Lesson

In my childhood home there were no healthy boundaries. The adults in my family routinely invaded each other's emotional and physical space, and mine.

While my mom could be loving and fun to be around, often it did not take much for her to flip from light to dark. Out of nowhere, she would become critical—especially of me, her oldest child. She blamed me for things, or criticized my actions, almost every day. I tried my best to be good, but it didn't matter. I had learned to suppress my own feelings of anger and never even tried to set a boundary with her.

I have many memories of my mom getting mad at me while I was helping her prepare a meal. She would say something critical, leave the kitchen, walk down the hall to her bedroom, and close the door behind her. As I watched her walk away, I would become frightened. As an adolescent, my sense of personhood was developing and in those moments it would vanish. I would go up to her bedroom door and ask if I could come in. She always said I could, and I would find her sitting on a chair in the corner. I would kneel on the floor in front of her and apologize. I recall a sense of begging for forgiveness. She would eventually forgive me and we would go back to what we were doing.

On a separate occasion, when my mom was standing close to me yelling angrily, she interrupted her harangue to say harshly, "And take that look off your face!" I'm not sure exactly what she saw on my face, but inside I felt tense and scared. From then on, when she was angry with me I concentrated on keeping my face serene despite my fear. My first priority was always trying to please her.

Then, in my late teens, I started to push back. I pushed back the same way she pushed me. No boundaries, no discourse, no respect. Just verbal attacks and counterattacks.

I left home when I was nineteen, but did not go far and continued to see my mom regularly despite our verbal altercations. She was my mom, after all, and there was more to our relationship than fighting. Then I got married, and when my husband and I were expecting our first child we moved to a town a few hundred miles away. I felt relieved that I would not see my mom as often.

Twenty years later, the relationship between my mom and me had not changed. We would usually do well for the first day and a half we were together, but then the fighting would start. I had begun to recognize the moment when she reached a tipping point. There was a slight change in her tone, a shift in her energy. Soon after that, she would explode at me and I would explode back.

I had been studying conflict resolution, though, and was determined to change my part of our dynamic. Before my mom arrived for her next visit, I arranged to stay with a friend during the visit if I needed to. I bought a cell phone so that I had a way to communicate if I left (this was before they were ubiquitous). And I rehearsed over and over what I would say to her when the shit hit the fan.

Sure enough, after a day and a half I sensed the familiar change in her energy. A few minutes later she blew up at me. I was in my home office, and she was standing in the doorway castigating me ferociously. This time, I did not react impulsively. Instead, I stood up, got my cell phone, and said to her firmly, "I'm leaving. Get out of my way." She stepped aside and I walked out.

I did not go to my friend's house, but I did walk around the neighborhood until I cooled down. When I returned home, my mom had cooled down too and we had a productive conversation about the issue that had aroused her anger.

That was when I realized I had a choice—I did not have to react to my mom's aggressive behavior in the familiar way. I could set a boundary instead.

Part VI

The Bridge is Here and Now

Chapter 18

Nowness

*"The only true thing is what's in front of you
right now."*

—Ramona Ausubel

Crossing the bridge, and expressing yourself authentically on your side of the bridge, are tools that help you to connect with what's going on right here, right now. The bridge itself only has meaning in the present moment. Even if you're talking about the past, the conversation itself is happening *now*. Simply noticing what's happening in the present moment is also a tool, a skill I'm calling "nowness."

If you're like most people, your thoughts and feelings consume a lot of your attention. Nowness is the willingness to take a step back from them and shift your attention to the larger landscape of the moment. You "show up" by expanding your awareness to include more of what's going on with you, with the other person, and in the dynamic between you.

In my real-estate days, one of my colleagues was an award-winning realtor whose name was Nathan. Nathan was professional in his demeanor and friendly with everyone. When I first joined Nathan's real-estate company, the workplace was being renovated and space was limited. Nathan generously offered to share his loft office with me until the renovations were completed. Unofficially, he was my mentor.

One day I wrote an offer on a property that was listed with Nathan. When I asked him for an appointment to present the offer to him and his clients, he asked to see the offer on the spot. I would have preferred to wait until the appointment, but I reluctantly handed it over.

I was surprised by Nathan's reaction. He became angry with me, saying that the offer was too low and that it would go nowhere. I had never seen him act this way. Although I felt flustered, I pressed for an appointment to present the offer anyway and he reluctantly agreed. An hour later we met with his clients at their home. By then, Nathan had collected himself and exhibited his usual professional demeanor. The offer presentation went smoothly.

Later that day I went back to the office. Although it was after hours, I noticed that Nathan was still there. What would I say to him? Although I felt inclined to pretend that his earlier outburst had not happened, I decided to break with tradition and "stand up for myself." This was before I had learned any communication skills, and I went overboard. As I neared the top of the stairs to our shared loft, I exploded: "How dare you talk to me the way you did? This is a perfectly reasonable offer! The property is overpriced anyway!"

Heated accusations went back and forth. In the midst of our argument, Nathan shifted gears. Out of the blue he shouted, "Do you want an apology? Alright, I'm sorry!" In a flash of insight he had realized what he was doing and had taken responsibility. This was his moment of nowness.

His words stopped me in my tracks and brought *me* back to the present. Although I was still angry, I chose to accept his apology and our shouting match was over. The next day, Nathan apologized again with greater sincerity. I apologized for my outburst and the tension between us evaporated. Indeed, the conflict and its resolution strengthened both our working relationship and our personal friendship.

Acknowledging the Unspoken

Many years ago I was out for a walk, ruminating on some personal drama. In the midst of my mental spin, I looked up and saw a brilliant, beautiful sunset that took my breath away. I have no idea what I was thinking about at the time, but I still remember that sunset.

Sometimes nowness means noticing a spectacular sunset, and sometimes it means noticing something less obvious but still important (like Nathan's moment of insight). In either case, nowness expands your perspective to include more of what's going on here and now.

In our communication with other people, spoken words are what we tend to pay the most attention to. But studies have shown that words make up only a small percentage of the total information being transmitted in face-to-face exchanges. Someone's tone of voice actually conveys more than the words themselves, and their body language carries the strongest message of all.

With nowness, you pay attention to all of it. When you notice that someone's body language is sending a message that is inconsistent with their words (or when there are no words at all), you can pause and say what you are observing in that moment. This can be followed by a question, by self-disclosure, or by a request (or by some combination of these). Here are some examples:

- "You're not saying anything, and I'm starting to feel uncomfortable. What are you thinking?"

- "You say that you're fine, but you've been pacing around the room. What's up?"

- "You're staring out the window, which makes it hard for me to talk to you. This conversation is difficult for me, and I'm guessing that it's difficult for you too. It would help me if you would look at me."

As these examples show, sometimes nowness means acknowledging your discomfort or someone else's. If there is an elephant in the living room, you do not walk around it pretending it is not there. You name it, and that becomes the new starting point for the conversation. When you call attention to the "elephant in the living room," though, be careful to describe only what you see or hear and avoid making accusations. By limiting your description to that which you can observe with your eyes and ears, you maintain a respectful tone that invites cooperation. Notice how the above examples demonstrate this use of sensory observation:

- "You're not saying anything." *(As opposed to "You're being sullen.")*

- "You've been pacing around the room." *(As opposed to "You are NOT fine.")*

- "You're staring out the window." *(As opposed to "You're not paying attention to me.")*

When someone's sole communication is through body language, or when their body language contradicts their verbal expression, it is important to tread carefully. They are using body language to communicate because they don't feel comfortable enough to verbally express their inner struggle. You might suggest a reason for their behavior, but do so using an "I" statement to acknowledge that it is *your* understanding and may not be true. ("I'm guessing that this conversation is difficult for you.") You are offering your interpretation as a way to move the conversation forward, not as a way to analyze or judge.

William

When William married Julie, Julie's twelve-year-old daughter Tanya entered his life full-time. William struggled to connect with Tanya. In the midst of conversations with Tanya, she would often seem to pull into herself. She would sigh, start tapping her foot, and look anywhere but at William. William would keep talking, trying to draw Tanya out. But nothing he said seemed to reach her.

Then William decided to take a different approach. When Tanya visibly disengaged from him, William gently named Tanya's behavior with statements like, "I noticed that you've sighed a few times" or "I've noticed that you've been looking away from me." When William said this, Tanya would smile awkwardly, start looking at William again, and eventually start talking.

By naming what he observed without judgment, William brought Tanya back into the conversation. He came to understand that her withdrawal was actually an invitation for him to gently come closer. Tanya just didn't know how to say it.

Practicing Nowness

In general, nowness is about bringing yourself back from wherever your mind has wandered. Hitting the pause button is all about nowness—you can only insert a pause *now*. Listening skills, too, can help you cultivate nowness as you keep returning your attention to something beyond your own perspective. Over and over, you drop your idea of what you think is happening and your habitual way of being, and return your attention to what the other person is saying.

"I" Language is also about nowness because you are describing your experience in the present moment. You are going beneath your thoughts, tuning into your felt sense, and giving voice to it. As I mentioned earlier, discovering and expressing my inner experience was an enormous shift for me. Training myself to do this meant that I had to pay attention in a whole different way. I had to look at what was going on for me *now*.

Nowness is beautifully expressed in the poem "The Baal Shem Tov" by Stephen Mitchell, which includes the following passage:

> *Prayer was*
> *a quality of attention.*
> *To make so much room*
> *for the given*
> *that it can appear as gift.*[xxii]

The present moment is always available to you, no matter where you are or what you are doing. In ordinary conversations, you might notice not only what the other person is saying, but also what is going on for you underneath the surface. Perhaps your silence is starting to feel uncomfortable. Perhaps you have asked so many questions that the conversation is beginning to seem like an interrogation. Perhaps you have said so much about yourself that the other person is losing interest. These insights can then inform the way you proceed in the conversation, enhancing your connection with the other person.

In the midst of conflict, when your emotions are strong, shifting your attention in this way can be difficult. When you insert a pause and bring your attention back to the present moment, though, the drama can lessen its grip on you. You are more likely to catch the concession that someone else is willing to make, or even their attempt at humor. But whether or not there is openness on their part, you, yourself, can shift gears. No matter how much you believe that you are right, you can pause, reflect, and use a skill.

Don

Don, a professional trainer, was leading a workshop. One of the participants in the workshop, Sharon, took offense to something he said. From Sharon's response, Don assumed that she had misunderstood him. He told her that he agreed with the point she was making. It was as though Sharon had not heard him. She made the same point again, and Don again replied that he agreed with her. He thought that would soothe her, but it didn't. Sharon continued to argue, becoming more and more agitated. Finally Don really listened to what Sharon was saying and said to her, "What I said was really upsetting for you." At that point Sharon gave an affirmative response, explained herself some more, and then was able to settle back into the workshop.

Don paid attention to what was happening *now* and adjusted his approach to suit the moment.

Saying Nice Things

Nowness is not just for moments of tension. When we bring our attention back to the present moment, sometimes (perhaps often) we see that things in our immediate world are just fine. It can bring us relief and joy to acknowledge this, even for a moment. And when the present moment shows us the kindness or generosity or loveliness of someone else, what a gift it is to tell them! Watch people light up when you congratulate them on their success or thank them for doing something for you.

Saying nice things is an essential component of healthy relationships. Like listening to someone with sincere interest, acknowledging their good qualities or good deeds helps them to feel seen and valued, and strengthens the bond between you. Stephen Covey refers to this as making deposits in their emotional bank account.[xv] Building a balance in this "account" not only strengthens the good vibe between you, it also makes it more likely that the account can withstand withdrawals you make down the road when the inevitable challenges come along.

Lightening Up

Nowness can take you by surprise. Once I was in a leadership position on a campaign working long hours, day after day. My supervisor, Franklin, felt that it was his duty to watch me closely. He demanded frequent updates and commented on every decision I made.

At some point, I realized that I was living through my personal version of hell. I felt alone, angry, and helpless. In a quiet moment I thought to myself, "OK, suppose this really *was* hell, where I would spend the rest of eternity answering to Franklin. What would I do?" Instantly, I knew the answer: I would lighten up. Later that day, during a telephone call with Franklin, I cracked a joke. Flustered, he hung up on me! Later, though, he returned the good humor and our whole relationship changed. We became colleagues instead of adversaries, working together as a team. I could hardly believe the transformation.

Life can be like that. When I open to the present moment, I realize that it is all I really have so I might as well relax and enjoy it. A bumper sticker catches my eye: "Forget about world peace. Visualize using your turn signal." The present moment calls me to slow down and pay attention. When I do this, anything is possible.

Part VII

Using the Bridge in Challenging Situations

Chapter 19

Difficult Conversations

*"One difficult conversation is better than a bunch of
conversations that avoid the truth."*

—simplykerry.net

In every long-term relationship, sooner or later people get crosswise
with each other. Issues come up that need to be resolved. When you
value the relationship, and you want to discuss an important issue,
how do you maximize the possibility of a positive outcome? How do
you navigate through the challenge in order to increase understanding
and come up with a solution that works for both of you? This chapter
lays out a strategy to do just that.

At the end of the chapter, there's also a discussion about how to
proceed when you disagree with someone (anyone) about a controversial subject. In a polarized world, this can be another form of "difficult
conversation."

Difficult Conversations About Relationship Issues

The following instructions form a general guideline for initiating
and navigating a difficult conversation about an interpersonal issue:

1) Make a preliminary request or remark.

2) Say one short, clear statement that expresses your main
point.

3) Stop.

4) Go to the other side of the bridge.

5) Bring the other person back to your side of the bridge.

6) Keep talking and listening until the conversation reaches a natural conclusion.

Let's go into more detail about each of these steps.

1) Make a Preliminary Request or Remark

The first step is to ask the person if this is a good time to talk. This gets their attention in a non-threatening way and lets them know that you have something important to say. It also gives them the opportunity to tell you if it's not a good time. If that's what they say, don't let that be an excuse not to have the conversation. Ask them when they will be available and arrange to talk with them then.

2) Say One Short, Clear Statement That Expresses Your Main Point

It's helpful to prepare and rehearse this statement in advance. Keep it short! This is just the beginning, not the whole conversation. If you say too much, they will likely stop listening. Important elements are:

- The "DE" Script (describe the behavior you want to address and its effect)

- *(Optional)* One or more of the following:
    — Your intention or preference
    — An acknowledgement of the other person's positive intent
    — Personal disclosure of your discomfort in raising the subject
    — An invitation for them to speak

These elements need not be expressed in sequence, nor must they all be included. Here are some examples:

- "When you re-assigned the job duties on your own *(describe behavior)*, I didn't understand your reasoning. I'm confused and concerned about the long-term effect of you making such big changes in our business *(effect of the behavior on you)*. I would like to discuss how we're going to move forward from here for the benefit of everyone *(your preference)*."

- "This is hard for me to say *(personal disclosure)*. Chantelle, I love you. You're my sister and I want the best for you *(your intention)*. When you start seeing someone who has hurt you so badly in the past *(describe behavior)*, I feel concerned that you're going to get hurt again *(effect on you)*."

- "When you talked about visiting your family for our vacation *(describe behavior)*, I felt a little uncomfortable *(effect)* because I was hoping to spend some time with just the two of us *(your preference)*. I also know how important your family is to you *(acknowledge their positive intent)*. Can we talk about this?" *(invitation for them to speak)*

3) Stop

Once you have made your statement, stop talking. Remember that you are not trying to convince them of your position, you are just starting the conversation. If the other person does not respond right away, let there be silence while they process what you have said.

4) Go to the Other Side of the Bridge

Eventually, the other person will likely respond. If not, you can ask them for their thoughts. Once they start talking, make a sincere effort to understand their point of view—their side of the bridge—using the listening skills described in Chapters 10 and 12. Suspend your own perspective while you try to understand theirs.

The time you spend on the other side of the bridge will vary depending on the intensity of the other person's reaction. In highly charged situations, you might find yourself over there for quite a while. Even though you initiated the conversation, for some period of time you will likely do more listening than talking.

5) Bring the Other Person Back to Your Side of the Bridge

Once you sense that the other person has said everything they need to say, and you have thoroughly acknowledged them, bring them back to your side of the bridge. As you share more of your perspective, use "I" Language. You could also incorporate any new information you learned while you were listening. If your ultimate goal is to request a change in behavior, this is when you can do that.

For some difficult conversations, your emotions might be strong. It's okay to say this. For example, you could say, "I feel upset and confused and I don't know what to do about it. I've wanted things to change, and I've been afraid to talk to you about it."

If it seems that things aren't going well and the skills are not working, then *use them more*. If you stick to the skills, at the very least you won't say something that you later regret.

It can also be helpful to insert a positive statement at some point, such as, "I value your friendship," or "I love you," or "I want to sort this out in a way that works for both of us."

6) Keep Talking and Listening Until the Conversation Reaches a Natural Conclusion

As you proceed, there is a good chance that the conversation will evolve into a dialogue. This is a good thing—it indicates that the two of you have made the shift from "you against me" to "you and me against the problem." Continue to use listening skills, though, and to ask open questions (e.g., "What do you think?") If you want confirmation that the other person understands what you are saying, ask them to tell you what they think your main point is.

Conversations like this can be time consuming, and you might be tempted to move things along by jumping to a conclusion or a solution. I encourage you to resist this impulse. Instead, take your time and let the solution emerge naturally. This makes it more likely that the other person will feel included. A solution you come up with together will be more satisfying, and enduring, for both of you.

Don't Take the Bait

In the course of any difficult conversation, the other person might attempt to bait you by saying something that will get under your skin. *Do your best not to take the bait.* Instead, pause and use the skills.

One way they might try to bait you is by asking a provocative question such as "Why are you making this so difficult?" While it is a social convention to answer questions, when you answer a question such as this you are giving away your power by letting them control the conversation.

Here are possible ways you can respond to a question such as, "Why are you making this so difficult?"

- Prompt *("Say more about that.")*

- Repeat back *("You think I'm making this more difficult than it needs to be.")*

- Reflect back the person's experience *("It sounds like you're frustrated.")*

- Reflect back the person's unmet desire *("You want this to be over with.")*

- Ask an open question *("What's going on for you right now?")*

- State your own experience *("I feel uncomfortable with that question.")*

Be careful not to say anything that could be construed as an answer to their question. For example, this is not a good time to state your intention. If you answer their question in any way, you are headed down the slippery slope of self-justification.

Doing Your Best is Good Enough

This guide is a general map for initiating and navigating difficult conversations about interpersonal issues. The key elements are to prepare in advance, keep your positive intention in mind, utilize all the communication skills you can muster, and be gentle with yourself before, during, and after the conversation.

It can be helpful to remember that conversations like this are, by nature, unpredictable. They have a life of their own, and they almost never go the way you planned.

You won't know the great things that could happen, though, unless you try.

Disagreements About Controversial Topics

Disagreements happen when we have different thoughts or opinions from someone about, well, anything. Sometimes we are deeply invested in our perspective, and they are equally invested in theirs. Such disagreements can quickly escalate into conflicts, but there is a better way.

If you find yourself disagreeing with someone and you feel your blood pressure rising, *hit the pause button* as soon as you realize it. Slow things down!

Having hit the pause button, you now have a choice. One option is to change the subject. Another option is to take a breath and proceed with the conversation for the purpose of finding common ground and sharing your own thoughts. For long-term harmony and mutual understanding, sooner or later it behooves us to venture into this uncomfortable territory.

Suggested steps for doing this are:

1) Cross the bridge by:

   a) Repeating back.

   b) Asking open questions to help you understand their perspective and their underlying values. You can also ask them about life experiences that led them to think the way they do.

   c) Reflecting back their experience if you sense they feel strongly about the subject. For example, you could say, "It sounds like you're really concerned about this."

2) Acknowledge anything they said that you agree with. You might share some of their fears or values, and/or there might be elements of their position that you think are worth considering.

3) Ask them if they would like to hear your perspective. You can say that you're hoping to find some common ground with them.

   a) If they show no interest in hearing your perspective, continue to listen or change the subject.

   b) If they say yes, share your perspective by:

      i. Using "I" Language as much as possible

      ii. Sharing relevant data and your personal experience

      iii. If they have stated something as a "fact," and you disagree that it is, indeed, true, you can say that you have a different understanding. State verified facts to support your position, including the source. If the other person challenges you on the things you say, acknowledge that disagreement. Also acknowledge areas about which you are unsure. Be as respectful as you can.

      iv. Continue the conversation, seeking understanding of their perspective and sharing your own. You are not trying to change their mind; you are trying to understand *them* and find out what you have in common with them.[xxiii]

In a polarized world, it can be tempting to avoid difficult topics or just talk with people who agree with us. While those are always options, I believe that we have to find a way to disagree better. We might even learn something along the way.

Chapter 20

Responding to the Dissatisfaction of Others

"I want to know if you will stand
in the center of the fire with me and not shrink back."

—Oriah Mountain Dreamer

While it is difficult to initiate and navigate difficult conversations, it can be even more challenging to be on the receiving end of someone else's dissatisfaction. When you detect someone else's negativity towards you, how do you manage your reaction? Following are different ways you can respond, depending on the situation and the degree to which you are triggered.

1) Curiosity
2) Listening
3) Apologizing
4) Self-disclosure
5) Silence

Let's examine each of these in more detail.

1) Curiosity

When someone expresses mild irritation, that's a good time to get curious. When I was a public agency hearing officer, the hearings were held in a conference room at the end of a hallway. Normally this passageway was well lit, but one time I was surprised to find it eerily dark—the hallway lights were out and there was barely enough light to find my way. I was concerned about how clients would experience this darkened hallway as I escorted them to their individual hearings.

I went into the office across the hall from the conference room and asked the person who worked there, Janice, what she knew about the lights. She said that the lights had been out all week, the situation had been reported, and she had no idea when they would be repaired. She seemed irritated with me.

Janice's reaction surprised me, for she was usually easygoing and warm. I felt a tinge of fear and started to withdraw emotionally. Then my training kicked in and I asked her, "Are you okay?" Janice replied that people had been asking her about the lights all week, and she was tired of answering questions about them. She just wanted the maintenance people to take care of it. She seemed relieved to express her feelings, and instantly I felt re-connected to her. I said, "So you're pretty frustrated about it." She replied, "Yes, indeed," and both of us shifted back into work mode.

Such a small thing, asking her if she was okay. And yet for most of my life it would not have occurred to me to do this. I have learned, though, that people's minor irritation is a signal to go further. The irritation is seldom about me, and if it *is* about me then it is usually something that is easily addressed. Displays of irritation are great opportunities to cross the bridge. The other person receives caring attention, and I learn information that helps me not to take it personally.

When in doubt, get curious.

2) *Listening*

Another option for responding to someone's negativity is to cross the bridge. It can be challenging to do this if their negativity is directed at you. But if you're able to maintain your cool, respond by using the listening skills described in Chapters 10 and 12.

If the other person's statement was brief or confusing, you could offer a prompt such as "Say more." If, on the other hand, their statement was complete and the meaning is clear, you could reflect back their experience. For example, you could say "It sounds like I've made things difficult for you," or "You're frustrated." As they continue talking, stay on their side of the bridge. Continue to listen, using all the skills, until they have finished expressing themselves. It is especially helpful to repeat back anything you hear them say more than once. Often, the better you listen the less time they will take to explain themselves.

Sometimes you might truly not understand the other person's concerns. If this is the case, after you have listened and reflected back, ask a question or two. Be careful to limit your questions, though, so that they do not turn into a counterattack.

Once you have listened thoroughly, respond naturally. You could offer an explanation or clarify an incorrect assumption. (If an apology is called for, see the next section.) If they are clearly upset and you do not know how to proceed, you could ask them "What do you want from me?" Asked with sincerity, this can be a powerful question.

There might be times when you are not able to address the other person's concerns for some reason. What you *can* do is say, "I wish I could help" (as long as it's true).

In other situations, a self-deprecating joke might be appropriate. Sometimes, laughter is the best medicine.

3) *Apologizing*

When you have made a mistake and the other person's dissatisfaction is a consequence of your actions, first let them say what they need to. After you listen well and affirm them, apologize.

Offering an apology as soon as they speak, without exploring their concerns first, does not usually work as well. Apologizing at the first sign of another's dissatisfaction can short-circuit the other person's process. You might find yourself apologizing again and again, hoping that it will make everything okay. You might as well be whistling in the wind.

When people are hurting or irritated, they need to be heard. Before they can truly accept your apology, they need to know that you see their pain. So let them say what they need to say and reflect back their experience. Then a single apology, said with humbleness and dignity, will usually do. A well-timed and heartfelt "I'm sorry" says it all.

There may be times when you realize that you behaved inappropriately after the fact, without the other person telling you. You might realize it yourself, or perhaps someone else brings it to your attention. Either way, you know that you need to attend to it.

This kind of apology has two parts. First, take full ownership of your behavior without making excuses. Second, say that you are sorry. For example:

- "Stanley, I spoke to you harshly yesterday. I'm sorry."
- "Geraldine, I made some assumptions about you that were untrue. I apologize."

If the other person accepts your apology, that is all that needs to be said. If the other person responds with emotion, go to their side of the bridge and stay there while they talk. Listen silently, then reflect back their experience to let them know that you understand how your actions affected them. Once they have had their say, you might need to apologize again, for the strength of their emotions might have prevented them from hearing you the first time. When appropriate, follow-up action might also be required for full resolution.

As is mentioned in Chapter 13, it works better to apologize for your actions than to apologize for their effect on others. Saying, "I'm sorry you feel that way" or "I'm sorry that you felt hurt" is not received well. It's much more effective to say, "I'm sorry for what I did," or "I'm sorry that I hurt you."

A sincere apology is healing for both you and the other person. If you have committed to some kind of action, and you proceed with it, that also helps. Even if some tension remains, it will usually dissipate over time. In the midst of your personal accountability, remember to be gentle with yourself.

4) Self-disclosure

When you have a strong emotional reaction to someone's negative comment, and you cannot sustain genuine interest in what they are saying, it is helpful to be honest about that. You don't have to pretend that you're okay. In fact, pretending that you're okay can perpetuate the conflict if your unexpressed emotions resurface later in a different form.

Once, in a telephone conversation with my friend James, I unknowingly said something that was hurtful to him. I then asked James a question and he replied with, "I'll answer your question in a minute, but first I have to take the knife out of my heart." James let me know, without blaming me in any way, how my words had affected him.

Here are some possible statements of self-disclosure:

- "I feel uncomfortable right now."
- "I'm feeling defensive."
- "Ouch" or "That hurt."
- "I'm having a hard time with what you just said."
- "I don't know what to say."

I have found it especially helpful to use the sentence, "I don't know what to say." When I feel at a loss for words, making this brief disclosure often helps me tap into an inner awareness. Then I know exactly what I want to say.

5) Silence

There is wisdom in the adage, "If you don't have anything nice to say, don't say anything at all." Your silence can protect you from yourself. Use it well—not to develop a simmering rage against the other person, but to go inward and attend to your defensive reaction. You can also ask yourself, "What part did I play in this?"

If you want to preserve the relationship, and especially if you want to heal it, long-term silence is not useful. Eventually, it behooves you to raise the issue with the other person using the process described in Chapter 17. Ask them if this is a good time to talk, make a straightforward statement about what occurred, cross the bridge, express your perspective, and proceed from there. Remember your desire to resolve the situation in a way that works for both of you, and say that at an appropriate moment.

When the Hurt Runs Deep

After my first marriage ended, I moved away from my family. My daughter Hayley, who was sixteen at the time, was very angry with me for leaving. During my calls and visits, she was often tense and critical. Moments of real connection between us were few.

I hung in with Hayley as best I could. I knew that my leaving had caused her immense pain, and that I had to bear the consequences of that while maintaining a level of self-care. Giving up was not an option. Eventually our relationship improved, with lots of learning and growth for each of us along the way.

We all have our own way of grieving and healing, and our own time frame for moving through that process. I knew I had to share Hayley's journey on her terms, not mine. This showed me that love is more than a feeling. It is showing up repeatedly for someone I have hurt, doing the best I can, and letting go of my desire for a quick resolution. Things change in their own way and their own time. People we love can be our greatest teachers.

Final Thoughts

When people express dissatisfaction with something you have said or done, you can ease the situation by crossing the bridge. This is not a time for you to try to correct them or fix them, as tempting as that may be. If you value the relationship, make an effort to understand them, to validate their experience, and to restore the connection between the two of you. If you just can't pull it off, do your best to pause and not lash back.

If you disagree with their perspective, try to wait until you have heard them out before expressing your own thoughts. They will be much more likely to hear what you have to say if they sense that you have tried to understand them.

Giving your care and attention to others who are hurting can be challenging, especially if their dissatisfaction is directed at you. Such is the journey of life.

So cut yourself some slack, and never give up.

Part VIII

Fruits of the Journey

CHAPTER 21

Autonomy

"In the middle of a difficulty lies opportunity."

—Albert Einstein

Many years ago, I drove to Washington D.C. to lead a workshop. As I was leaving D.C. to return home, I could not figure out how to get out of the city and onto the freeway. This was before GPS, and my paper map offered little help. After wandering around in search of a route, I found myself at a T-intersection where the street abutted a wide boulevard. There were cars parked on both sides of my little street, creating a narrow passageway to my left. I could see the freeway in the distance but had no idea how to get there. I eased the car forward, peering left and right, trying to get my bearings. As I did so, the front of my car protruded slightly into the intersection.

Soon a taxi came down the boulevard from the right and signaled to make a left turn onto my street. The driver had to swing wide, slow down, and maneuver carefully to get by my car. When our vehicles were closest to each other, he looked at me angrily and yelled an obscenity through his open window.

Then he was gone. I sat unmoving, stunned. I felt frightened and guilty, instantly believing that I had done something terrible and deserved his anger—my familiar "freeze" reaction.

I gathered myself, found my way to the interstate, and began the ten-hour drive home. Over the long day of driving, I contemplated the taxi scenario over and over. Several hours into the drive, I started to see that I had become hooked by a patterned reaction of self-blame. This led to an astonishing insight: *I do not deserve to be treated badly, even if I have erred in some way.* While I am accountable for my actions, I am not responsible for, nor deserving of, another person's aggression. For me, this was huge.

Accountability and Autonomy

What does it mean to be accountable for my actions yet not responsible for how others react to them? To be accountable for my actions is to say, "Yes, I did that" and to pay attention to how my actions impact others. By easing my car forward into the intersection, I had created a challenge for the taxi driver. I could own that.

Assuming responsibility for his anger, though, was something else. His anger was his, not mine. But taking responsibility for others' anger was ingrained in me, and that day it took many hours of reflection to shift my perspective. Even now, my initial reaction to others' anger is often to feel responsible for it. But I am not.

This also applies to situations in which I have truly hurt someone through my words or actions. Even then, I can take responsibility for what I did, and accept the natural consequences, without internalizing the other person's emotional reaction and taking responsibility for it.

I am not you. I am me.

Mandala Principle

A mandala is a symmetrical image used in some religious traditions. Secular mandala images abound—for example, in adult coloring books and on the internet. A mandala is round or square and is often ornate. In Tibetan Buddhism, the mandala principle represents the relationship between center and fringe.

Here is one example of a secular mandala:

I was well into my communication skills training when I realized that I could view my lived experience as an ever-evolving mandala. Further, I saw that consciously placing myself at the center of this mandala would be empowering for me. I also saw how little I had been doing that. Instead, much of the time I had been allowing my reactivity and my fear to determine my behavior. I realized that placing myself at the center of my mandala required me to overcome my reactivity and my fear, and act with intention.

What I feared more than anything was disconnection from others. What I wanted more than anything was to be fully myself, beyond my reactivity. Being at the center of my mandala meant risking disconnection in order to be myself, "feeling the fear and doing it anyway."[xxiv]

This is what it means to inhabit the center of my mandala and to conduct my life from that place of personal autonomy. Increasing my ability to do this has been slow going for me, with many backslides. Along the way, I have learned that I don't have to choose between being myself and staying connected with others. I can do both. I can love, and be loved, as a whole, imperfect, human being. Who knew?

Discovering Autonomy Through Communication

Experiencing personal autonomy is an ongoing, lifetime journey for me. My path with communication has been an integral part of this journey. When I started listening to others with the intention to understand them, I started really hearing what they were saying instead of my *idea* of what they were saying. This helped me not to take things so personally, and I became less reactive. The less I allowed my inner reactivity to drive my behavior, the more autonomy I had.

When I learned how to express myself more authentically, I began taking responsibility for my words, actions, and feelings. I also learned how to express dissatisfaction without rancor or blame, to ask for what I want, and to set boundaries. These abilities, by their very nature, help me to become more autonomous. I gained greater power and agency— more of a feeling of being my own person.

I find my autonomy in each moment by showing up, communicating in the best way I can at that moment, learning from my mistakes, and letting that be enough.

Sally

Sally knew that she was physically safe in her marital home, and that her husband Mark genuinely cared for her. But she and Mark were having frequent, intense verbal conflicts about many aspects of their life together. Entire weeks would go by when they barely spoke to each other except to yell. Sally felt self-righteous and indignant, blaming Mark for their troubles.

As much as Sally blamed Mark, somewhere inside herself she knew there were ways in which she, too, was contributing to the conflict. She received support from friends and engaged in self-reflection and self-care. Over time, Sally began to recognize that her self-righteous stubbornness was making things more difficult. Once she had that humbling insight, she shifted her approach to their difficulties. Instead of holding onto being right, she opened to her love for Mark and really owned the truth that she wanted it to work out between them.

The next time Mark poked at her verbally, Sally took a breath and chose to stay engaged in the conversation but not fight. By doing this she made it easier for Mark to look at himself as well. Over time, the tension between them diminished significantly.

Sally learned that she did not need to win the fight. She just needed to show up for herself and for Mark and see what happened from there. By stepping into her autonomy, she empowered herself and made room in her life for Mark to show up too.

Contemplating Forgiveness

When someone says or does something I don't like, even if it's minor, I often spend a lot of time ruminating on it. Forgiving them can be a way to release my sense of grievance and move on. So when I'm hanging onto a complaint about someone, eventually I ask myself, "Is this something I could forgive them for?" Even just asking myself the question releases me from my preoccupation, empowers me, and re-establishes my sense of our shared humanity. I do it for myself, not for them. Almost always, my answer is "Yes."

If I am feeling deeply wounded, though, forgiving someone is not so easy. Forgiving them does not happen just because I want it to or because I decide that it is time to forgive. But if I hold the intention to forgive and keep reminding myself of that when I slip into feeling powerless, I can gradually reclaim a sense of personal agency. That gradual process might go on forever. Sometimes my work is to forgive myself for being unable to forgive another.

The Courage to Be Yourself

Embracing our autonomy can be terrifying, especially for those of us who felt chronically helpless, unloved, or frightened as children. To experience my autonomy, I needed courage—not the brash courage of a Hollywood action hero, but the open, resilient courage of a warrior of the heart. In communicating differently, it took courage for me to face my discomfort and proceed anyway. That's why the technique is called Courageous Communication!

It was like learning any new discipline. At first, I had to concentrate on the skills and remember to use them. This was harder when I felt angry, ashamed, or frightened. As I became more familiar with the skills, I remembered them more easily and they became my normal way of communicating.

As time went by, I no longer succumbed to every feeling. I still felt the feelings, but using the skills gave me something to do that was intentional rather than automatic.

Courageous Communication helped me to find my voice.

Chapter 22

Compassion

"Our human compassion binds us the one to the other—not in pity or patronizingly, but as human beings who have learnt how to turn our common suffering into hope for the future."

—Nelson Mandela

In my understanding, compassion is more than a feeling. It is recognizing the suffering of another human being and taking action to alleviate that suffering. You can also have compassion for an animal, or for a group. You can even have compassion for the planet.

Recognizing suffering is the first component of compassion. It means tuning in, *seeing* their pain and letting it touch you. Allowing yourself to be touched is different from being overwhelmed. You feel a connection with the other person while maintaining a sense of your personal autonomy.

The second component of compassion is taking some kind of action that is appropriate for the situation. There is a sense of "stepping up," of acting with care and agency. There can also be a sense of surrendering to a larger view. Your action could arise from the question, "What wants to happen here?"

True compassion strengthens the connection between you and someone else while empowering both of you. Your care motivates your action, and your action reinforces your care. The other person is aided in a way that strengthens them. You don't rescue them or fix them; you serve them and in so doing you serve yourself.

In this way, compassion is a journey. It's also a way of life.

Crossing the Bridge as a Tool of Compassion

For me, and for those who receive training from me, the journey of Courageous Communication begins with showing up for others by crossing the bridge. In one communication workshop, a participant asked me if he had to care about people in order to use the skills he was learning. I replied, "No, you don't. But if you use the skills, you *will* start to care about people."

After I said this, I realized it was true—everyone I knew who used the skills, including myself, cared more about others as a result. People came into focus for me as separate individuals with lives and stories of their own. And once I understand someone's story, compassion flows naturally. My actions stem from genuine connection with them and not from my own ideas projected onto them.

Self-Compassion

Self-compassion is the willingness to extend the same care to yourself that you have for others. It helps you connect with your own humanity and "lightens your load."

Being gentle with yourself is one aspect of self-compassion. It means noticing your own uncomfortable feelings and creating an internal sense of care for them. When you experience the urge to rationalize, dismiss, or judge what you're feeling, or to blame someone else, you can notice that too. As best you can, you love the place inside yourself that is hurting, angry, or scared. And, as best you can, you forgive yourself.

Another aspect of self-compassion is the exercise of your personal agency by asserting yourself. This can mean setting a boundary, asking for what you want, or expressing yourself in some other way.

These aspects of self-compassion—loving yourself and asserting yourself— together provide a foundation for compassionate action in the world. By attending to yourself with care and presenting yourself with clarity, you are strengthening your ability to be present with others. And being present with them is a first step in alleviating their suffering.

Joaquin

Joaquin had a difficult relationship with his supervisor, Michelle, who consistently criticized his work. He felt uncomfortable around her and avoided her whenever possible. Realizing this, Joaquin decided to take a different approach and cross the bridge. When Michelle came into view, he approached her rather than retreating. He asked her about her children, her weekend activities, and similar topics. Michelle's demeanor changed when Joaquin reached out to her in this way—she visibly relaxed and warmed to him.

By reaching out to Michelle, Joaquin expressed his autonomy *and* his care. And to the extent that Michelle's negativity had been an expression of her tension or discomfort, Joaquin's sincere interest helped to alleviate it. *This is the essence of compassion.*

Being With Someone Who is in Emotional Pain

When you are with someone who is feeling sad or is hurting emotionally in some other way, you might be inclined to assure them that they will feel better soon, or offer advice, or even suggest that it is time for them to get over it and move on. You might try to bypass their emotions and fix the situation. If one of these approaches is familiar to you, you are not alone. Most of us respond to others' emotional suffering by trying to make it better. It's difficult to be with someone who is hurting!

I've come to understand that my desire to make it better is really about alleviating my own discomfort in the presence of their suffering.

And yet, just being with them, and not trying to make it better, is often the very best thing I can do for them.

When people are in emotional pain, what they might want more than anything is to be accepted or loved as they are at that moment. As much as they might prefer to feel better, the healing has to come from inside and they often resist your efforts to help them. More often, what they want is for you to show up for them, "bearing witness" to their real experience of suffering.

In other words, compassionate action might not feel like much action at all. But by listening silently, or acknowledging someone's felt experience, or holding their hand, you are giving them permission to feel what they feel so they can do their own inner work and healing. You cannot short circuit that process, nor can you do it for them.

At an appropriate time, it might be fine to say, "I wish I could make this better for you." But *trying* to make it better almost always backfires. The best thing you can do for them is to remain steady and keep your heart open, despite your own discomfort.

If you can do this, after a time you might be inspired to do or say something that seems to arise naturally out of the fullness of the situation. At these times you are no longer motivated by a desire to relieve your own discomfort. And when you act, you're not invested in the outcome. This kind of action can be genuinely helpful to them.

In my career as a prison chaplain, I sat with many people during their dark times. On one such occasion, I was with a young man named Alfonso, who had recently come to prison for the first time. In the process, he had lost everything. He was overwhelmed by his new circumstances and felt unsure of how he would go on. I sat with him in my office for a long time, doing a lot of silent listening and acknowledging his feelings. Through my words and actions, I let him know that I was there for him with no judgment or expectations.

When it was time for Alfonso to leave, I walked him back to his housing unit. When we got there, before I turned to go I looked him in the eye and said, "You will get through this." If I had said it earlier in the conversation, I would have pushed him away. But because I had stayed with him as he suffered, he was able to hear my final words of encouragement. I knew I had helped him and that he would, indeed, find a way to go on.

Boundary Setting as Compassionate Action

While setting a boundary with someone is about having compassion for yourself, it can also be helpful to the other person.

Several times, my friend Kim asked me for advice about how to assert herself in an ongoing difficult situation with her boss. Each time, I made suggestions which she did not follow. Instead, Kim chose to say nothing to her boss and just wait until the difficulty blew over. I felt frustrated. The next time Kim called about the same situation, I reminded her about our previous conversations and said that I would not offer any advice. I also reminded her that the situation was passing and that she would likely feel better again soon, as had happened before. Kim was upset and hung up. I felt shaky. It was difficult for me not to try to help my friend.

An hour later, I received an email from Kim apologizing for ending the conversation. Kim said that she needed to gather her courage and address the situation on her own. She also said she understood my unwillingness to give her advice that she might or might not follow.

I did not have the ability to make Kim do her own inner work—we never do. But by declining to give her advice one more time, I had saved myself from frustration and had provided an opportunity for her to reflect on her own inner process. Because she chose to do this, my boundary setting turned out to be good for both of us.

Opportunities Abound

Opportunities for compassionate action present themselves frequently in our lives, whether we recognize them or not. Just use the skills! Simply by crossing the bridge with someone, you might be easing a burden that you didn't even know about.

At other times, someone's suffering is apparent. Your compassion might be more intentional, and the rewards might be more visible as someone relaxes in the caring space you create for them. At still other times, taking care of *yourself* might be the most helpful thing you can do.

In whatever form it takes, your compassion makes the world a better place for all of us.

Chapter 23

Presence

"You've gotta dance like there's nobody watching,
Love like you'll never be hurt,
Sing like there's nobody listening,
And live like it's heaven on earth."

—William W. Purkey

The word "presence" means showing up fully in the present moment for ourselves and others. Being present is especially challenging when we feel uncomfortable or vulnerable, and yet that's when it's most important. Life brings us many opportunities to cultivate presence.

One such opportunity arose for me when I led a series of classes on "Working with Conflict" at a conference. The three hundred conference participants were educated, thoughtful people who shared a sincere desire to open their minds and hearts. Many of these people were my personal friends. I had been anticipating the conference with a mixture of excitement and fear—I wanted to make a good impression.

In the first of my three presentations, I talked about the importance of crossing the bridge in a conflict in order to understand the other person's point of view. I then presented some active-listening skills and led several listening exercises.

At the end of the class there was a brief time for questions. The first person who came to the microphone said that she was familiar with these skills on the receiving end—they had been employed by workplace managers to manipulate her. The experience had made her highly suspicious of the skills, and she had no desire to use them.

I responded to her by talking about the importance of one's intention. I said that it is important to use the skills with a sincere interest in the other person's perspective, not just as a way to placate or manipulate them. In fact, I told her, the skills themselves would help her to cultivate interest in others if she used them sincerely.

Then a second person told a similar story, then a third. I continued to stress the importance of one's intention. By this time there was a buzz in the room. The session came to an end, but there was no sense of completion. People were clearly aroused by the discourse.

For the remainder of that day, many people avoided me while others approached me to offer their support. The people who supported me were concerned that the others were not "getting it," and encouraged me to persevere. As for the ones who were avoiding me, well, I could only guess what they were thinking because they were not saying it to me. In a short period of time, I had become the focal point of—that's right—a conflict.

As I contemplated the best way to proceed with the classes, I came up with several clever things to say that would surely convince people of the usefulness of the skills. But then I had a conversation with my colleague, Paul, who had presented other material before me. Very gently, Paul pointed out that I had become defensive at the end of the class and had not been fully present with people as they tried to tell me about their experience with the skills. I had not crossed to their side of the bridge, and they were rebelling.

What a shock! Here I was, the "expert" on working with conflict, and I had not practiced the very skills that I was teaching. I had not listened to understand what it was like to feel manipulated by the skills. It was one of the most humbling experiences of my life.

When I began the next session, I acknowledged my defensive reaction at the end of the previous class. I invited people to come forward with their concerns about the skills and said that I was now ready to hear them. I stated the obvious—that we were in the midst of a conflict about conflict. The good news is that one can always have a fresh start.

From that point on, people relaxed. I relaxed, too. We had a genuine, heartfelt discussion. In the final session I presented more skills and everybody did role plays in small groups. As far as I could tell, most people had learned some things and appreciated the classes.

For myself, I had been through the fire. It was my worst nightmare come true. Sitting in front of these people, my friends, I felt ashamed and vulnerable. And I survived. I had learned that you really can begin again. I had also learned that vulnerability can be both excruciating and powerful. Our strength lies not in our cleverness or our wisdom, but in our willingness to remain present in the midst of our discomfort.

Bon Voyage!

When I was a youth and a young adult, I was certain that most people did not like me. The truth was, I did not like myself. I did not even *know* myself! The skills of Courageous Communication prompted deep soul searching and massive changes in the way I showed up for myself and others. I learned how to give up control and be vulnerable, and I learned that staying with my vulnerability helps me to be more present no matter what is going on around me. Contacting my vulnerability also enabled me to understand myself better and to be more gentle with myself.

Now I know that most people *do* like me, and I like myself a whole lot better. I'll never be perfect, and it doesn't matter. I'm good enough as I am.

May these skills help you find your way through your own challenges, and may they enrich your life as much as they have enriched mine.

It only takes one person to change the tone of a conversation or a relationship, and that person could be you.

Afterword

*"I do not at all understand the mystery of grace—only
that it meets us where we are but does not leave us
where it found us."*

—Anne Lamott

Late in my mom's life, I visited her in her home. My sleeping spot was a sofa in the living room, and I was keeping my suitcase in her bedroom. One morning I had converted my "bed" back to a sofa, and we were sitting there chatting. After a while, she got up and went into her room to write in her journal, closing the door behind her. Soon afterward, I realized that I needed something from my luggage. I went to her bedroom door, knocked softly, and gently opened it. Mom looked up from her writing, sighed, and said, "I wanted some privacy." I said I was sorry, got my item, and tiptoed out closing the door as I left.

A few minutes later, Mom came out of her bedroom. She said, "I have been doing that to you for your whole life. I don't know why I get so irritated with you over such small things. If anyone else had interrupted me, I wouldn't have minded. But with you, I have always minded. I'm sorry."

I was blown away. I felt validated in a way I had never experienced, and released from an internal construct that had defined me as far back as I could remember. I did not recognize the depth of its hold on me until her words loosened its grip. I was not a bad person after all, and her anger was never my fault.

One comment cannot undo a lifetime of conditioning, and that was not the last time Mom criticized me. Even still, in that moment my whole perspective shifted. I had a new, brighter outlook. Mom had *seen* me. She had crossed the bridge to my side and recognized the impact of her actions.

We never know what's coming, and sometimes it's good.

Acknowledgements

To my instructors at the School of Health, Community, and Social Justice at the Justice Institute of British Columbia, I owe an enormous debt of gratitude. It was there that my journey with conflict resolution began (when it was called The Center for Conflict Resolution Training). Special thanks go to two instructors whose impact on my life will never be forgotten: Kelly Henderson, who first opened the door for me with such kindness, and Elizabeth Azmier-Stewart, whose wisdom helped me to find my way.

Sakyong Mipham Rinpoche was a reference point of wisdom and compassion for me for many years. He led me into the teachings of Buddhism, a path that continues to inform my life. I would also like to acknowledge the many teachers of Shambhala Buddhism, too numerous to name, who guided me in the principles of fearlessness and gentleness.

I completed writing the first draft of this book then put it away for nineteen years. I have lost touch with most of the early readers, and I am aware that some have passed on from this life. Even still, I would like to acknowledge their support and assistance. Thanks go to Suzanne Allen, Karen Butcher, Susan Gillis Chapman (who was the first to suggest the book title I ended up using), Neil Chethik, Zoe Drake, Janet Jernigan, Kim Massey, Alan Moore, Lee Schulz, John Stempel, Jeannie Trudel, Hayley Watson, and Brother Lawrence at the Abbey of Gethsemani. Psychotherapist and author John Wellwood gave many thoughtful comments on the first section of the book. Sandra Kryst reviewed the entire manuscript and made many helpful suggestions.

Following the completion of the first draft of the book I became a prison chaplain, a position I held for sixteen years. During that time I developed and taught a program for inmates based on the skills presented in this book. I would like to thank my supervisor, Stuart Young, for his unqualified support of this program. I would also like to thank the many inmates who learned these skills and applied them, reminding me of the value of this work and helping me to hone my own understanding. Special thanks go to Ezekiel Salazar, who co-facilitated the program with me for many years.

Coming back to the book after nineteen years was a whole new adventure. I would like to thank my coach Karl Hebenstreit, who told me unequivocally to revive the book and *publish it*! Lone Subryan provided support and transformative advice on how to think about the writing process. She told me to "just tell your story." And that's what I did.

Words cannot convey the depth of my appreciation for my "book doula," Sallamah Aliah, who helped me to find my voice with insight and skill. Her deep understanding of the material and her wise counsel made the book immeasurably better. I am also grateful to readers Steve Ghan and Kristie Persinger, my beloved sister. Both Steve and Kristie provided valuable perspectives and excellent feedback chapter by chapter as this version of the book took shape.

My gratitude goes to others who read the completed manuscript and whose feedback helped to hone it—Bill Cahill, Carmine Hanks, Susan Havlina, Jennifer Keller, Michele Lonergan, and Julie Worley. Michele offered a valuable therapist perspective, and Jennifer gave many thoughtful suggestions that enhanced the book's structure and its autobiographical content. Jennifer helped me take "just tell your story" to a whole new level, especially in the Preface.

In one thoughtful sentence, Yvonne Boyd gave me what I needed for the subtitle of the book.

My gratitude also goes to the many clients and friends who shared their stories with me for inclusion in the book. Special thanks to Freddie Myles, whose story is a shining example of the power of these skills.

My mother, Donnie Wilson, provided support and encouragement at every step of the way. Although she has passed from this life, her lifelong quest to learn and grow continues to inspire me.

To my partner, Reginald Johnson: thank you for exploring with me the many facets of communicating well in the context of a healthy, loving relationship between two imperfect beings.

The Skills of Courageous Communication

1) PAUSE!

2) State your intention *(Chapter 9)*

   When a situation is starting to deteriorate, or when it seems that you are being misunderstood, state your intention. A good statement of intention to memorize and use is:

   "I want to sort this out in a way that works for both of us."

3) Skills for crossing the bridge

   a) Listening *(Chapter 10)*

      i. Silent listening—listen without saying anything

     ii. Prompting—open invitation for the other person to say more

    iii. Repeating back—repeat back some version of what you heard them say

        • Paraphrase—say it in your own words

        • Exact words—repeat back word for word

    iv. Summarizing—encapsulate the essence of what the person said

   b) Deeper listening *(Chapter 12)*

      i. Reflecting back their experience—acknowledge what you think they might be experiencing

       ii. Reflecting back their unmet desire—acknowledge what you think they might be wanting

  c) Things to be careful about or avoid *(Chapter 13)*

       i. Interrupting

       ii. Saying, "I'm sorry you feel that way."

      iii. Giving advice

      iv. Saying, "I understand."

       v. Describing a similar experience of your own

      vi. Agreeing

     vii. Using the word "but"

  d) Open questions *(Chapter 14)*—begin questions with who, what, when, where, how, or (sometimes) why

4) Skills for expressing yourself

  a) "I" Language *(Chapter 15)*—begin sentences with the word "I" and use Language of Experience (say what you are experiencing rather than what you are thinking)

  b) Expressing dissatisfaction *(Chapter 16)*—use two or more steps of the "DESC" Script

       i. Describe the behavior in neutral language

       ii. Effect of the behavior

      iii. Specify the preferred behavior

      iv. Consequence for them if the unwanted behavior continues

  c) Saying "No" and setting boundaries *(Chapter 17)*—express yourself clearly and firmly

5) Nowness *(Chapter 18)*

  a) Pause and bring your attention back to the present moment, then say what you observe in the other person or in yourself

b) Say nice things

c) Lighten up

6) Skills for Heightened Situations

a) Difficult conversations *(Chapter 19)*

    i. Make a preliminary request or remark

    ii. Say one short, clear statement that expresses your main point

    iii. Stop

    iv. Cross the bridge

    v. Bring the other person back to your side of the bridge

    vi. Keep talking and listening until the conversation reaches a natural conclusion

b) Disagreements about controversial subjects *(also Chapter 19)*

    i. Cross the bridge

    ii. Acknowledge anything they said that you agree with

    iii. Ask them if they would like to hear your perspective

- If they say no, continue to listen or change the subject
- If they say yes, express your thoughts
- Then continue the conversation, seeking understanding of their perspective and sharing your own.
- Acknowledge differences as you look for common ground.

c) Responding to the dissatisfaction of others *(Chapter 20)*

    i. Curiosity—ask them about their concern or complaint.

   ii. Listening—cross the bridge to understand more about what they're saying.

 iii. Apologizing—after you cross the bridge, offer an apology.

 iv. Self-disclosure—if you're too triggered to cross the bridge, say so.

  v. Silence—if you've absolutely reached your limit, don't say anything at all.

Exercise: Reflecting Back Experience

Give reflective responses to the following statements. Possible responses are shown on the next page.

1) "This is not what I expected."

2) "Now that Sam is off to college, I don't know what to do with myself."

3) "How could you do this to me, after everything I've done for you?"

4) "This has been the most amazing day of my life."

5) "That movie rocked!"

6) "My ex-wife just got arrested for drugs and the kids have come to stay with me. I don't know how I'm going to manage."

7) "Eight months till I retire. I can't wait!"

8) "What is wrong with her?"

9) "What is wrong with you?"

10) "I'm trying to tell you something important and you're not listening!"

11) "It's not worth working hard around here, nobody cares."

12) "I wish I hadn't said anything."

Possible reflective responses to the statements on the previous page:

1) "This is not what I expected."

   Possible reflective response: "You're surprised" or "You're disappointed."

2) "Now that Sam is off to college, I don't know what to do with myself."

   Possible reflective response: "It sounds like you're feeling pretty lonely."

3) "How could you do this to me, after everything I've done for you?"

   Possible reflective response: "You feel betrayed."

4) "This has been the most amazing day of my life."

   Possible reflective response: "You're happy!"

5) "That movie rocked!"

   Possible reflective response: "You really liked it."

6) "My ex-wife just got arrested for drugs and the kids have come to stay with me. I don't know how I'm going to manage."

   Possible reflective responses: "You're really going through it right now."

7) "Eight months till I retire. I can't wait!"

   Possible reflective response: "You're looking forward to whatever's next."

8) "What is wrong with her?"

   Possible reflective response: "You're upset about what she did" or "You're concerned about her."

9) "What is wrong with you?"

Possible reflective responses: "You're upset about what I did" or "You're concerned about me."

10) "I'm trying to tell you something important and you're not listening!"

Possible reflective response: "You sound frustrated."

11) "It's not worth working hard around here, nobody cares."

Possible reflective response: "You're feeling discouraged."

12) "I wish I hadn't said anything."

Possible reflective response: "You're regretting it."

Exercise: Reflecting Back the Unmet Desire

Give reflective responses to the following statements by saying your best guess for the unmet desire. Possible responses are shown on the next page.[11]

1) "Eight months till I retire. I can't wait!"

2) "There's no telling what he'll do next."

3) "I'm trying to tell you something important and you're not listening!"

4) "It's not worth working hard around here, nobody cares."

5) "This is driving me crazy! She never answers the phone, and she doesn't call me back!"

6) "They were so disrespectful to that person!"

7) "My father's health is declining, and his doctors can't figure it out."

8) "I'm bored!"

9) "My daughter is spending too much time on social media."

10) "You would think that something so simple wouldn't be so time-consuming."

11) "There's no end to the drama."

12) "It just doesn't make sense."

---

[11] You usually have a choice about whether to reflect back the feeling or reflect back the unmet desire. In this exercise, try to name a possible unmet desire.

Reflective responses to the statements on the previous page, suggesting a possible unmet desire:

1) "Eight months till I retire. I can't wait!"

   Possible reflective response: "You want to get on with the rest of your life."

2) "There's no telling what he'll do next."

   Possible reflective response: "You want to know."

3) "I'm trying to tell you something important and you're not listening!"

   Possible reflective response: "You want to be heard."

4) "It's not worth working hard around here, nobody cares."

   Possible reflective response: "You'd like more interest and support from management."

5) "This is driving me crazy! She never answers the phone, and she doesn't call me back!"

   Possible reflective response: "You want to make contact with her."

6) "They were so disrespectful to that person!"

   Possible reflective response: "You wanted them to show some respect."

7) "My father's health is declining and his doctors can't figure it out."

   Possible reflective response: "You want him to get better."

8) "I'm bored!"

   Possible reflective response: "It sounds like you want some excitement in your life."

9) "My daughter is spending too much time on social media."

   Possible reflective response: "You'd like her to do other things."

10) "You would think that something so simple wouldn't be so time consuming."

    Possible reflective response: "You want it to be finished."

11) "There's no end to the drama."

    Possible reflective response: "You'd prefer it if things were to settle down."

12) "It just doesn't make sense."

    Possible reflective response: "You want to understand."

Exercise: Open Questions

For each closed question, give an alternate open question. Possible alternate open questions are shown on the next page.

1) "Will you be here on time?"

2) "Did John do this?"

3) "Isn't this painting beautiful?"

4) "Did you go to the movie?"

5) "Have I hurt your feelings?"

6) "Were you with Joe when it happened?"

7) "Don't you just love that book?"

8) "Was that made in China?"

9) "Is it round or square?"

10) "Did you have fun on your vacation?"

11) "Do you want pizza for dinner?"

12) "Do you love me?"

Open questions you could ask instead of the closed questions on the previous page:

1) "Will you be here on time?"

   Possible open question instead: "When will you be here?"

2) "Did John do this?"

   Possible open question instead: "Who did this?"

3) "Isn't this painting beautiful?"

   Possible open question instead: "What do you think of this painting?"

4) "Did you go to the movie?"

   Possible open question instead: "Where did you go?"

5) "Have I hurt your feelings?"

   Possible open question instead: "How are you feeling?"

6) "Were you with Joe when it happened?"

   Possible open question instead: "Who were you with when it happened?"

7) "Don't you just love that book?"

   Possible open question instead: "What do you think of that book?"

8) "Was that made in China?"

   Possible open question instead: "Where was that made?"

9) "Is it round or square?"

   Possible open question instead: "What shape is it?"

10) "Did you have fun on your vacation?"

Possible open question instead: "How was your vacation?"

11) "Do you want pizza for dinner?"

Possible open question instead: "What would you like for dinner?"

12) "Do you love me?"

Possible open question instead: "How do you feel about me?"

Exercise: "I" Statements

For each statement, give an alternate "I" statement using Language of Experience. Possible restatements in "I" Language are shown on the next page.

1) "That was a great dinner!"

2) "You spend too much money."

3) "This food is terrible."

4) "You never listen to me!"

5) "It's too noisy in here."

6) "You're driving me crazy."

7) "You keep contradicting yourself!"

8) "This doesn't concern you, so don't even ask about it."

9) "Can't you get your life together?"

10) "Why do you treat me like that?"

11) "You're ignoring me."

12) "They're just being stubborn."

Possible restatements in "I" Language of the statements on the previous page:

1) "That was a great dinner!"

   Possible "I" statement instead: "I enjoyed that dinner!"

2) "You spend too much money."

   Possible "I" statement instead: "I'm concerned about our finances."

3) "This music is terrible."

   Possible "I" statement instead: "I don't like this music."

4) "You never listen to me!"

   Possible "I" statement instead: "I want you to hear me."

5) "It's too noisy in here."

   Possible "I" statement instead: "I would prefer it to be quieter."

6) "You're driving me crazy."

   Possible "I" statement instead: "I feel frustrated."

7) "You keep contradicting yourself!"

   Possible "I" statement instead: "I'm confused."

8) "This doesn't concern you, so don't even ask about it."

   Possible "I" statement instead: "I would prefer not to talk about it."

9) "Can't you get your life together?"

   Possible "I" statement instead: "I'm concerned about you."

10) "Why do you treat me like that?"

Possible "I" statement instead: "I don't want to be treated like that."

11) "You're ignoring me."

Possible "I" statement instead: "I feel ignored."

12) "They're just being stubborn."

Possible "I" statement instead: "I'm having a hard time with them."

Brown, Brené, *Rising Strong: How the Ability to Reset Transforms the Way We Live, Love, Parent, and Lead*, Random House, 2017

Covey, Stephen, *The Seven Habits of Highly Effective People*, Simon & Schuster, 1989 & 2004

Gottman, Julie Schwartz PhD & Gottman, John PhD, *Fight Right: How Successful Couples Turn Conflict into Connection*, Harmony, 2024

Neff, Kristin, *Self-Compassion: The Proven Power of Being Kind to Yourself*, HarperCollins Publishers, 2011

Noll, Douglas E., De-escalate: *How to Calm an Angry Person in 90 Seconds or Less*, Simon & Schuster, 2017

Remen, Rachel Naomi, "Helping, Fixing, or Serving?" Lion's Roar, 25 October 2021

Ruiz, Don Miguel, *The Four Agreements*, Amber-Allen Publishing, Inc., 1997

Schulz, Kathryn, *Being Wrong*, HarperCollins Publishers, 2010

---

[i] Quote widely attributed to Milarepa, an 11th century Tibetan meditation master: "When you run after your thoughts, you are like a dog chasing a stick: every time a stick is thrown, you run after it. Instead, be like a lion who, rather than chasing after the stick, turns to face the thrower. One only throws a stick at a lion once."

[ii] Victor Fleming (director), *The Wizard of Oz*, Metro-Goldwyn-Mayer, 1939

[iii] "Sad and tender heart" is a variation of "the genuine heart of sadness" and is a term I learned from Chögyam Trungpa's teachings. See *Shambhala: The Sacred Path of the Warrior*, Shambhala Publications, Inc., 1984

[iv] Pema Chödrön, Buddhist teacher and author, popularized the term "getting hooked" in this context. See Chödrön, Pema, "How We Get Hooked and How We Get Unhooked," *Lion's Roar*, 13 January 2023

[v] Frankl, Viktor, *Man's Search for Meaning: An Introduction to Logotherapy*, Simon & Schuster, Inc., 1959

[vi] Stephen Covey found this quote in a library book but did not note the name of the book (and could not find the book when he returned to the library to look for it). Covey thought that the quote beautifully summed up the teachings of Viktor Frankl.

[vii] Rainier Maria Rilke, *Letters to a Young Poet* (Stephen Mitchell translation), Random House, 1984, 2001 Modern Library Edition, p. 34 (original italics)

[viii] Ref. www.berkeleywellbeing.com/attribution-theory

[ix] "Don't Take Anything Personally" is the second of Don Miguel Ruiz's "Four Agreements." See Ruiz, Don Miguel, *The Four Agreements*, Amber-Allen Publishing, 1997

[x] Elie Wiesel, "Tanner Lecture on Human Values at Snow College," 22 May 2006

[xi] When I wrote the first draft of the book, I attributed "Nevertheless, I will dance" to Elie Wiesel, Holocaust survivor, author, and Nobel Peace Prize Laureate. When I came back to the book, I looked online and was not able to find any attribution to Elie Wiesel nor to anyone else. This short sentence speaks to me, though, so I'm using it anyway and claiming it for myself.

[xii] According to Wikipedia, the author of this prayer is unknown. Although it is attributed to St. Francis of Assisi, it is not included in the "Prayers of St. Francis" of the Franciscan Order. The prayer first appeared in 1912 in a small French spiritual magazine called *La Clochette* (*The Little Bell*), published by a Catholic organization in Paris named *La Ligue de la Sainte-Messe* (The League of the Holy Mass). The author's name was not given.

[xiii] Steven R. Covey, *The Seven Habits of Highly Effective People*, Simon & Schuster, 1989 & 2004, p. 247

[xiv] Harriet Lerner, *The Dance of Anger: A Woman's Guide to Changing the Patterns of Intimate Relationships*, HarperCollins Publishers, Inc., 1985, pp.14-15

[xv] See the Glennon Doyle podcast, *We Can Do Hard Things*

[xvi] I believe that I heard this story from Pema Chödrön, but it is not in any of her writings or interviews. The story is used with permission from The Pema Chödrön Foundation.

[xvii] Quote is attributed to Carl W. Buehner, a high-level official in the Mormon church, in *Richard Evans' Quote Book* compiled by Richard Evans, Publisher's Press, 1971

[xviii] This story, too, is unsourced. I believe that I heard it from Pema Chödrön but it is not in any of her writings or interviews. The story is used with permission from The Pema Chödrön Foundation.

[xix] This quote is often attributed to Theodore Roosevelt, but no known source can be found to verify the attribution (per the Theodore Roosevelt Center at Dickinson State University).

[xx] While this statement has been made by many famous people, its origin has never been identified.

[xxi] Stephen Mitchell, *Parables and Portraits*, HarperCollins, 1991

[xxii] Steven R. Covey, *ibid.*, pp. 215-234

[xxiii] These instructions are adapted, in part, from material from *Braver Angels* (braverangels.org)

[xxiv] Susan Jeffers, *Feel the Fear and Do It Anyway*, Ballantine Books, 1988

Trime Persinger *(Tree-may)* is a relationship coach with more than twenty-five years' experience helping people to communicate with clarity and courage.

During her sixteen-year career as a prison chaplain, Trime developed a communication-skills training program for Adults in Custody, *The Art of Communication*, for which she received an Outstanding Service Award from the Oregon Department of Corrections.

Trime holds a Certificate in Conflict Resolution from the Justice Institute of British Columbia and an M.Sc. (Bus. Admin.) from the University of British Columbia. She is a Certified Narrative Enneagram Practitioner.

She has two amazing children and three extraordinary grandchildren. She lives in Richland, Washington and she loves to hike!

Learn more at trimepersinger.com.

www.ingramcontent.com/pod-product-compliance
Lightning Source LLC
Chambersburg PA
CBHW051426130726
47987CB00005B/1927